THREE THOUSAND MILES
TO FREEDOM

THREE THOUSAND MILES TO FREEDOM

BRIG MARKANDAN MURUGESAN PILLAI, MC

Lancer • New Delhi • Frankfort, IL
www.lancerpublishers.com

LANCER

Published in the United States by

The Lancer International Inc
19558 S. Harlem Ave., Suite 1,
Frankfort, IL. 60423.

First published in India by

Lancer Publishers & Distributors
2/42 (B) Sarvapriya Vihar,
New Delhi-110016

© Col Ravi Pillai 2009

All rights reserved. No part of this publication
may be reproduced, stored in a retrieval system or transmitted,
in any form or by any means, electronic, mechanical, photocopying,
recording or otherwise, without the prior permission of the publishers.
For additional information, contact Lancer. Printed at Sona Printers, New Delhi.

Printed and bound in India.

ISBN-13 : 978-1-935501-21-3 • ISBN-10 : 1-935501-21-6

Online Military Bookshop
www.lancerpublishers.com

IDR Net Edition
www.indiandefencereview.com

CONTENTS

	Preface	7
	Prologue	9
1	Entering the Prison Camp	17
2	Crossing Malaya	33
3	Through Siam	47
4	The Burma Grind	61
	Epilogue	135

PREFACE

My father wrote this first in the form of a report from notes he made during and soon after his return to India.

Some years later he was prevailed upon to convert the notes and the report into a book for publication.

This is the book he delivered.

Unassuming and modest to the core he did not see himself as having been particularly brave or heroic.

We, his sons, saw him for the essential being he was — open, cheerful, liberal, with a strong sense of humour and literature inclined — a brown sahib who insisted that two drinks a day were the secret to longevity.

Truly liberal and secular, he was a creature of his circumstances — his rationality came from his engineering background, his love of English and Tamil literature from a love of reading.

We therefore, often did not recognise the toll on his physical and mental health that captivity in and escape from Singapore to India had taken.

He hardly ever spoke of the bouts of bullying and torture that he and other prisoners had often encountered.

He engaged with life cheerfully every morning and took it as it came.

It was a philosophy and an attitude that he carried through to the end of his life. He chose to see the best in people always; never took himself too seriously — with every day a fresh slate to write upon.

For me — one of his sons, his essential humanity was reflected in his love of engaging with people and his capacity to look at a mirror and see an image he could mock and laugh at.

What I enjoyed most in assisting with bringing this book out was that I could see him in action in each of the pages that I read. It is an easy read and I trust that some of you will see the same qualities in the reading of what is a short history of an event of the Second World War that has not lost its lustre with the passage of time.

Thanks are due to my mother who oversaw the transition of a manuscript to the book it has become today. Thanks are also due to all others who have contributed in the making of this book.

Ravi Pillai
10 September '09

PROLOGUE

On the night of February 15, 1942, the second most stunning event of the Second World War took place, an event that stood next only to the Pearl Harbour bombing in its shock effect. Singapore fell. We, the Allies, stood defeated by the conquering forces of Japan. The Malayan Campaign came to an end at 2000 hours, though sporadic firing continued till the middle of next day. The civilians had gone into hiding, and this pearl of an island, Singapore, lay shattered, plundered of its splendour. Soon, the Japanese would come and march us soldiers off to prison camps.

And now, as dawn shed its first dim light on the new day, the 16th, I felt a slight ray of hope and the strength of resolution. I decided to escape, come what may. This book is an account of my escape from a prison camp in Singapore. It took me six months after that fateful day, but in mid July, I arrived at the General Headquarters in New Delhi, India.

I was the first eyewitness to arrive with any account of the Japanese occupation of Malaya, conditions in prison camps and the state of some occupied countries of Asia in general.

What partly encouraged me to think about escaping was an experience I went through earlier in the campaign, before the surrender. I once found myself surrounded by the Japanese. But somehow, having slightly disguised myself, I managed to follow the enemy troops marching ahead for four days, slipped through their lines and finally rejoined my unit. Little did I know that in less than three weeks I was again to fall into the hands of the enemy. Since this escape was not very difficult, I began toying with the idea of making a get away from the island. I had at that point no concrete plans about how to go about it or where to go. All I knew was that I had to cross enemy territory somehow and slip into Allied lands.

Determined not to spend the rest of the war behind barbed wire, I sought permission from my unit's Commanding Officer (CO), Major Robert Dinwoodie, to make a run for it before the Japanese came. Had I escaped on 15 February, when there was general confusion all round, it might have been a little easier and faster. But, being a soldier new to such a situation, I thought the right thing would be to seek the CO's permission. Major Dinwoodie's realistic response managed to douse the fire in my belly for the time being and I came out richer by $30. He pointed out that Singapore to India 'was a hell of a long way off' and the journey and the road pitted with hazards. "In any case", Dinwoodie said, "You can't escape now." He had forwarded a list of survivors to the Japanese and warned that if I escaped they might execute the unit's other officers. Rumours that the Japanese decapitated prisoners on the flimsiest pretexts had been rife. Finding, however, that my mind was made up, he made a generous contribution of $30, all he had at the time. But he insisted that I should take the unit under my charge until we were officially imprisoned and then think of escape.

Thus on 16 February, we were marched off to a place cordoned off by the Japanese for our 'reception'. Here prisoners were divided into groups for various camps in Singapore. Bidabari Prison Camp was the one allotted to my unit. On way to the camp, I was lucky to find two books lying on the road, which I quickly picked up and pocketed. One was a thick volume *On The Run* containing escape stories by gallant men during World War I. The other was an Atlas in excellent condition. On 18 February, we arrived at the prison camp where I would spend the next few months.

The living condition in the camp went from bad to worse and the fatigues we were put through increasingly strenuous. As a diversion, I began reading *On The Run*. Each day, the conviction kept growing stronger inside me that I must make my escape as early as possible. I therefore made an effort to get to Sumatra by the sea. But the courage of desperation I had mustered till then, gave way to stark fear when, just when I started to swim, I saw in the moonlight sharks gamboling in the sea. The prison conditions, I said to myself, was for the moment preferable to being swallowed alive. Thus my freedom this time ended in less than a day when I slipped back into the camp unnoticed. Sumatra fell a few days later. The sea was written off as my escape route. The only option that remained was the land route.

The destination I had in mind at this stage was somewhere in Burma or Chungking (Chongqing) in China. The whole of Malaya, Siam (Thailand) and possibly even French Indo-China (Vietnam) lay between freedom and me. It became apparent that, without precise, detailed preparations, any attempt at escape would most certainly end in disaster. My first step in this direction was to invest a third of the $30 to find a reliable contact outside, a civilian.

First, to chart out the route, it was essential to memorise the names of the chain of villages and towns I would pass through. And then plan a second and even a third alternative should any particular route have to be written off. Here the Atlas I had picked up came in very handy. It was also evident that most of my journey would have to be in the good old fashion of the infantry — just trudge along on my two feet. I therefore started at once on a regimen of strict mental training and hard physical exercises so that I would be completely fit to meet any eventuality.

I was trying my best to garner as much information as I could from the Atlas and, at the same time, began hardening my feet by walking bare foot around the camp as much as possible. The regimen took some time to produce effect. So far, no news of the civilian contact had reached me. By now, Rangoon too had fallen to the enemy. My destination, therefore, was narrowed down to some place in China. I was now rapidly memorising the names of the places on the possible routes and hardening my feet. My camp mates, watching me absorbed in the pursuit of these odd habits, firmly concluded that I had passed the realm of sanity. This did not worry me very much, except for an occasional doubt that they may just be right. I found that I had more and more time completely to myself.

Things were not smooth sailing in the prison camp. It was quite a common occurrence for some prisoners to disappear from working parties. They tried to merge into the crowd of civilians. Most of these, if not all, invariably returned voluntarily to prison camps under different names, as the conditions in the city happened to be no better and escape from the island well nigh impossible.

At that time, the idea of organising the prisoners to form a 'Force' against the Allies was gradually being given a concrete shape by the Japanese. For one, prisoners were made to choose between joining the Japanese Independence Force (JIF) and, going into a concentration camp. As a preliminary step towards the latter, I was moved with about 3,000 others into a separate camp. I was convinced that escape could not be postponed much longer. I was the officer-in-charge of the provost duties in the new camp.

All I needed at this stage was to walk into any friendly civilians' house if there was one; the rest of the plan was clear in my mind. I was very anxious to get my hands on some sort of a medical haversack to take with me on the journey. I obtained some help from my medical colleagues. I was able to collect a very large number of Atebrin (anti-malaria) pills.

By now I had contacted my civilian friend, one Radhakrishnan, who not only offered financial assistance but, was also anxious to join me if there was any certainty of my reaching India. I could not give him this guarantee. Convinced of my determination that nothing short of death or very serious illness would stop me, he insisted that I take him along.

The plan was to leave the camp on the 6th of May. My friends in the camp, at considerable personal risk, agreed to try and cover my absence for four days, the period by which I expected to be clear of Malaya.

There was a rude shock in store for me at this stage. I was one of the officers detailed by name to attend a propaganda lecture on 7 May. It would become impossible, therefore, for my friends to cover my escape even for one day. They were convinced that chances of escape were very small indeed, and so pressed me to give up the attempt. My plans were made. I did not want to make a last minute change and decided to take the risk. I left the camp on 6th May at about 2100 hrs.

I shall not go into very great detail of the eventful journey with my civilian friend here. We crossed in to the mainland of Malaya under the nose of the Japanese and the identification party, which they had detailed to cover all exits from the City. How we obtained passports from Japanese Army Headquarters at Penang, how we dodged the Siamese immigration authorities, how a Japanese consulate gave us passports for entry into Burma, are merely the workings of chance in our favour. We were lucky enough not to be caught while travelling as stowaways in a little fishing boat upto Mergui from Victoria Point. Mergui onwards it was mostly a case of dodging the Burmese dacoits and walking up North.

We found the will to march for days under starvation conditions, but the acid test was keeping our wits about when confronted by the Japanese under those conditions. It was sheer good fortune that the Japanese headquarters at Monywa should give us the benefit of the doubt after three days of continuous interrogation. The same headquarters gave us a pass and put us on board a troop boat going towards Kalewa. The rest of the journey was almost uneventful.

The use of the Atlas, the anti-malaria pills and the hardened feet surely made things much less difficult. Being Asiatic was a great advantage for both of us. A westerner could not have merged into the local population in the "Far East".

The need for a high degree of physical fitness for this type of venture will be appreciated if I mention, that, Radhakrishnan never quite recovered. He succumbed to the ravages of the journey and died in August 1945, three years after entering India.

1

ENTERING THE PRISON CAMP

I have been told many times that I was very lucky. I suppose I have been born under lucky stars. Looking back into my past, as far as I can remember, I am unable to list any great regret or serious cause for complaint. But these lucky stars seem to have a kink in their pattern. I say this because, invariably, it has always taken quite a long time for my dreams and ambitions to be realised.

I was born in a village in Tirunelveli, near Cape Comorin in South India. Till I was ten years old I had very little knowledge of places beyond my district. Yet, before I was twenty, I had travelled widely within India, and had been to almost every big cantonment in North India. It was not surprising that I had grown to love the uniform and the stirring tunes of martial music.

My eldest brother was my guardian, provider and the example that I followed. He was very keen that I should take up law as a profession and made this clear in many ways. In deference to his wishes, I refrained from expressing openly my desire to join the army.

When I was barely sixteen years old, I presented myself for

recruitment into the University Training Corps. Much to my regret and chagrin, I was not accepted, as I did not meet the corps' minimum physical requirements. The lecturer in charge of recruitment without even bothering to take the necessary measurements, dismissed me with a curt "not you" and went on to the next boy in the line. I moped around for the next few days, wearing a hangdog look. But soon I bounced back and started exercising in the gymnasium. By the time I was in my second year at the University, my chest had filled out, weight gone up and I had grown taller by a couple of inches. I felt very proud, feeling I had achieved all this by the dint of my hard work. It might well have been that, I had attained the minimum physical standard through natural process of growth more than anything else. But I wanted to believe that my efforts were rewarded. I could not join the University Training Corps in the second year as well, because of a rule that only boys in junior classes could be enrolled.

After I had graduated with mathematics and physics, I was asked to join Law and M.A. classes. By that time I had become a little bolder in discussing my career plans with my brother. I explained to him that I did not wish to join the Law College. But, by then, I was too old to join the Indian Military Academy at Dehradun.

The Academy was considered a little too distant by the people in Madras. Also, there was a general impression that a career in the army needed more brawn than brains. Despite his connections in the army circles, my brother had never thought of advising me to enter the army. Possibly the fault was mine, because I never openly showed my desire to join the army and now it was too late.

ENTERING THE PRISON CAMP

When the Second World War broke out in September 1939, I was in Lahore and I realised that I had been given another opportunity. Without any delay I went to the Office of the General Officer Commanding (GOC) Lahore District and made enquiries. One Major Hathaway, who was then DAA & QMG, had a few minutes to spare for me. As advised by him, I entered my name in the Volunteers Register. Mine was the first name.

Within a couple of months, I was asked to report at the District Headquarters and was asked whether I would like to join the Cavalry. I had expressed earlier a preference to the Corps of Engineers. The need for Cavalry officers appeared more urgent than for Engineers. I decided, however, to wait for a call from the Corps of Engineers.

On 01 September 1940, almost one year after the outbreak of war, I reported at the Headquarters of Royal Bombay Sappers and Miners, Kirkee, for pre-commission training. The training was to be for six months and if I did satisfactorily, I was due for commissioning on 1 May 1941. We were a varied bunch of 20 cadets, some English men from tea plantations, an Australian, an Irishman, and six Indians. After the first three weeks, two of the Indians left and there were only 18 cadets in the class. I suppose I was one of the youngest. I did not mind that one bit. But what worried me more was my physical status. I was often teased on that account, mostly in just good fun, but sometimes it was just not funny.

Our Sergeant Instructor in Weapons Training (WT) and Drill, by the name of Woodward, was very competent and self-confident. He was held in high esteem. The fact that I was lean and at least one and half inches taller than him did not prevent him from having a few jokes at my expense. Thanks to my four years training with the 2nd Urban Infantry Battalion of Bombay ITF and my determination, I finished my WT and Drill with some credit. The last four months was smooth sailing. I had made some good friends amongst the cadets. They were quite unconcerned by the fact that I was short.

I was commissioned as a Second Lieutenant on 24 February 1941, a few weeks ahead of the original schedule. My first posting in the army was to 45 Army Troops Company, which was being raised and due to go overseas shortly. By mid March '41, we were on the high seas aboard HMS *Devonshire*, trained and equipped for the campaign in the Western deserts. We had altered course near the Suez Canal. Thereafter, we maintained a steady course southeast. We were obviously heading for Singapore, though our destination was a secret.

While on board *Devonshire* I was shifted to the sick bay with a severe attack of malaria. I had not recovered even when the ship touched the Singapore Port. The units disembarked and moved to their respective destinations. I was carried out on a stretcher, and an ambulance took me to Queen Alexandra Military Hospital. When the time came for my discharge, the kind Commanding Officer gave me three days casual leave. I enjoyed this leave — sight seeing in the city and cruising on a motor launch in the Straits. Being in a strange land, and with no friends, I got tired of Singapore and was eager to get back to my unit.

The day before my departure from Singapore, I met a Tamilian in a South Indian coffee house. After hesitating a little, he came over to my table and within a few minutes we realised that we had much in common. We were both engineers on foreign soil. In no time we were friends and he invited me to dine at his house. I spent the night at his place. He was living alone, his family having moved to India a few months before. He saw me off at the railway station. During our brief stay together he made enquiries about life in the army. May be he was thinking of joining the Services. I had a feeling he was a little envious that I was in the army. We were destined to meet again within a year. And then, it was I who was envious of his status.

In the meanwhile, the 45 Army Troops Company had moved up country to a place called Mantin Camp just south of Kuala Lumpur. I had no difficulty in picking up the threads of life in an army unit as things were still in the process of settling down. Then followed a period of intense excitement. We were full of enthusiasm and all our energies were directed to improving the training in the unit.

We had some amenities to while away our spare time. The planters, as we soon realised, ran efficient establishments and were excellent hosts. Service officers were always welcome to their homes. I was the only Indian officer, and yet I had no occasion to feel that there was any colour discrimination, barring one instance.

Singi Ujong Club was essentially a plantation club, but located in the town of Seremban. Occasionally, Services officers were invited to the club. On one occasion, when an invitation was being extended to me, my Commanding Officer cautiously advised me to be careful. I took the hint. I turned down the invitation. But I cannot deny that I felt hurt. I found it strange that, even though I could sit at the same table with the planters in their own homes and, what is more, sit at the dining table at the Government House because I wore the uniform, I could not attend their club. It might have been that such clubs were deemed superior, or the Government House had to remember its obligations to Services officers, or at any rate keep up appearances of doing so.

The unit had barely settled down when it was moved by train to the state of Kelantan, a single railway line providing the only means of entry by land into that state. There was no road linking Kelantan with the rest of Malaya. The unit set to work making concrete pillboxes and gun emplacements near the main bridges on the railway line. We spent three months cut off from civilization, except for the few trains that passed by daily.

During my stay here I accompanied a retired Chief Conservator of Forests, who was possibly the only white man to have befriended the primitive Sakai tribes that lived deep in the jungles of Kelantan. I was very fortunate in having been able to observe the Sakais in their jungle camps. These people were a happy lot, even though they lived a primitive life in the fever-ridden jungle, roaming about almost naked, just not bothered about modern paraphernalia like clothes.

When the defences along the railway bridge were complete, we returned to Mantin Camp towards the end of October 1941. We soon picked up the threads of services' social life in the area. One started to hear that the Japanese were aggressively on the march forward. We, especially the young officers, dismissed such talk as rumours and were convinced that 'the

Japs would get a good hiding if they stuck their neck out too far'. Of course, as things were to turn out, we were just 'putting up a good front' and indulging in a lot of wishful thinking.

I recalled this empty boast when we soldiers in Malaya were being scattered like dry leaves by the Japanese whirlwind. The concrete pillboxes we constructed with such care and expense were not used at all.

On 5 December 1941, I was seeing a film in Seremban when the show was interrupted with slides ordering all ranks to return to their camps immediately. I found my camp humming with activity. On 6 December at dawn, our unit was sent marching to a village, Kron, on the Siamese (Thailand) border. We reached Kron by midday on 8 December only to find that the battle had already broken out.

Kron Call (ad hoc brigade) of which we formed the sapper component, was given the task of advancing some 40 miles into Siam to a defile known as the Ledge and construct a defensive position so as to stop enemy advance into Malaya from this direction.

The advance was progressing fairly satisfactorily. The unit had drawn blood. The air was tense, but nevertheless we kept smiling. It looked as if the way we said farewell to friends on 5 December, 'see you in Tokyo', might prove prophetic. We were within sight of the Ledge but could not reach it. The enemy was already there with a large number of medium tanks. Later, we came to know that Kron Call Brigade was the only formation which had captured vast areas. The rest of the army in Malaya had been put on the defensive right from the commencement of the Campaign. By 11 December 1941, it was clear that we had no chance. The withdrawal that commenced on that date was to stop only with the fall of Singapore two months later.

The details of the Malayan Campaign are public knowledge today. What is not known is the difficult and significant role played by the engineer units in this theatre. The enemy had immense superiority in air and armour. They were at home in the jungles — we were scared of the woods. The sappers were shunted about much more than any other troops. Worse still, more often, they found themselves preparing obstacles in the face of the enemy with no protection parties. That the Japanese advance was so rapid was not on account of inadequate or faulty demolitions. Most of the obstacles remained uncovered by our firepower. There were many Sapper officers in this theatre who had blown up bridges not only when the enemy was closing in on the far bank, but more often when the Japanese were right on top of the obstacle.

The lot of the 45 Army Troops Company was worse than any other Sapper unit. We were sent post haste all over the mainland of Malaya far more than any other unit. From being part of the 9th Infantry Division (Inf Div) South of Kuala Lumpur, almost overnight we ended up at Kron. When Kron Call was absorbed in to the 12th Brigade, my unit was shunted out to augment engineers of the 11th Infantry Division at the Sungei Patani Bridge.

We were at the defensive position of Chemor, Ipoh, Bidur, and Kampar. Hardly had these last positions been abandoned when we were off to operate the Jerantut ferry. Back at Kuala Lumpur, we were busy in demolishing bridges north of the town as well as the railway tunnel. Soon we were at Parit Sulong Bridge. Though we were lucky to have two platoons of the NORFOLKS protecting us while at work, the threat from the Japanese was high, as they were pressing us hard from Muar, while another enemy formation had cut our communication lines to the Headquarters.

A detachment of my unit entered Singapore for the second and last time on 31 January 1942. No one thought of it as a safe haven, but the reality was worse than our worst fears. The Island was besieged. The enemy was bombing the town indiscriminately and the water Supply system was under threat. I was in charge of the sapper contingent, entrusted with the tasks of finding alternative sources of water and the destruction of unexploded bombs.

While engaged on one of these tasks I found myself near the residence of one Radhakrishnan, a 34-year old teacher of engineering — the only civilian acquaintance I had on the island. I found him safe but thoroughly scared. It was either the 4th or 5th February 1942. I did what I could to assure him that civilians would be safe in Japanese hands. He was anxious to know what would be the fate of us soldiers. When I answered that we probably would be shot like stray dogs in the streets, I had no intention of indulging in melodrama. I did believe that our end would be in that fashion. We had repeatedly been warned to be ready for street-to-street fighting till the very end. My second visit to the residence of Radhakrishnan was very brief. Finding all other matters beyond personal safety were of virtually of no importance, we had very little to discuss. I was soon busy with my duties.

10th February 1942 saw Sapper activities come to an end. My unit along with two other engineer units formed an infantry battalion, which was tasked to defend a hill feature. The following four days were really the worst of the campaign. Many of our men were wounded and killed, in attacks on our defences. Out of the seven officers with the unit, three were wounded, and one killed on the spot. By the afternoon of 5th February, we had been dislodged from our defences, and we began to organize our defence in a built-up area, with the enemy being less than 200 yards from us. We felt we had reached the end of our tether, and indeed we had.

At about 8.30 p.m., the Commanding Officer gave his final orders to the officers left with the unit. The army in Malaya had capitulated. Our resistance was to cease forthwith. We were to remain in the same area. Next morning all arms and ammunition were to be stacked close by till the Japanese came and took-over. We were to apprise our men how to conduct themselves during captivity and that further orders would come in due course from the Japanese. Stunned by this momentous announcement, we went about doing things, that we had been directed to do, in a mechanical and perfunctory manner.

The men, I am sure, received this news with a sigh of relief for, whatever their condition was, they were still alive. Little did they realise then what prolonged captivity could do to a man. Even amongst the officers there was some hope that the Geneva Convention would protect the prisoners of war. Many British officers must have had serious forebodings as to what would happen to them in the next few days. Soon, there formed little groups of three or four, each talking in excited whispers.

I found myself beside two colleagues. We seriously thought of making a dash for the seashore under cover of darkness, stealing a boat and launching it out to sea. Once we cooled off, we saw that the idea was full of holes. We were some miles away from the seashore and anything could happen before we reached there. There was no guarantee that we would reach there without interference. Even if we did, there was very little chance that the troops already close to the sea would have left any boat for us. The most forbidding prospect was that once at sea, Japanese coastal patrols or aircraft would in all probability sight us. Convinced that there was no avenue left for escape, we decided to lie down on the roadside and get some sleep.

I lay down to sleep, but could not. I was wide-awake the entire night. Recent events of my life kept disturbing my mind. I thought of various incidents in the campaign — how I managed to dodge the enemy earlier on. With merely six other men on a 15 cwt truck, I had made wide detours along little known tracks and had rejoined my unit after three days. At Parit Sulong in Malaya, when surrounded by the enemy, I had abandoned all equipment except arms and light ammunition and, after wandering through enemy dominated territory, had rejoined own forces after four days. I was getting more and more determined that I should break away from the unit. If immediate escape by sea to Sumatra was not possible, I thought I should try to get away and get absorbed in the civilian world. There were thousands of Indians, and many from my part of the world and I, therefore, did not expect serious difficulties in getting some assistance from them. If only I could contact Radhakrishnan, I thought, I could plan something. I was not certain whether he was safe and alive and, even if he were, whether he had changed his residence.

The next morning, as I gathered my wits, I found that despite not having slept a wink, I felt no fatigue. I took David Edgar, the second-in-command of my unit, into confidence. He was full of encouragement for my resolve to escape. However, when he informed the Commanding Officer, his reaction was the first big dampener to my enthusiasm. He had two main objections: first, that Singapore to Kirkee (my depot) was 'a hell of a long way off', and second, and more important reason, was that he had included my name in the list of the survivors at the end of the Campaign. He told me that the list was on its way to the enemy and, if the Japanese found I had got away, they might behead all other officers of the unit. Such fears, justified or not, had been haunting the minds of us officers for some time.

I was fully aware of the vast distance from Singapore to India, but I believed that the risk I was taking was personal and did not affect anyone else. The last few words of my Commanding Officer were: "You, as the only Indian Officer, have to take over the unit and report to the Japanese. You may make any attempt at escape from your prison camp. I, however, sincerely advise you not try anything rash or foolish". Caught in a jam, I had to shelve the idea of taking flight. Very soon a Japanese soldier arrived. I was standing all by myself, anxiously looking at the house of some South Indian in the vicinity, casting envious glances, and wishing that I was in that house in civilian clothes. The Japanese soldier was approaching me and I soon realised he was intent on acquiring all the valuables I had on my person. I emptied my pockets and handed over the articles willingly, which included my fountain pen and all the cash I had. Finding his eyes riveted on my gold wristwatch and gold chain, I handed over both without any resistance. He was very greedy. He wanted the diamond ring I had on my hand as well. I would have given it, but unfortunately the wretched ring could not be removed. My gesticulations to show that my spirit was willing, but the flesh unyielding, did not cut ice. He took out a pocketknife and tried to open out the ring causing me considerable pain.

Luckily, a Japanese Officer came on the scene. I called for his assistance and fortunately for me, he spoke English and was indeed an officer and a gentleman. He beat up the looter and insisted on my taking back whatever he had collected. I found I was being given three wristwatches of which only one was mine and all the cash. Despite my protests, this officer insisted on my taking the lot, which I did. The soldier, who had robbed and injured me, slunk away the poorer for his attempt.

Instructions had been sent ordering the unit to proceed to Farrer Park. We had dumped all arms, ammunition, and other war related items such as compasses, binoculars, and maps. All vehicles were to be left behind except the one in which we were allowed to carry what was left of our rations. The unit arrived at Farrer Park on the afternoon of 16th February to find that most of the 45,000 Indian Prisoners of War (POWs) had already arrived. Strangely enough, I did not see a single Japanese guard. I learned that Singapore had fallen a month ahead of Japan's targeted date and they were just not prepared to handle thousands of prisoners.

There being no prison atmosphere, my obsession to make a break from it, returned. I met Colonel Bhonsle, who thought it was a good idea and encouraged me to get away as soon as possible. His only request was that I should communicate with his wife in India if I arrived there safely and assure her that he was alive, though a prisoner of war. I readily agreed.

On the night of the 16th of February, I slipped away and without much difficulty, reached the beach. My plan was to swim across by stages and find shelter in Sumatra, some 60 miles away. There was nothing fantastic or foolish in this idea, as there are some 100 islands in that stretch of 60 miles, and the maximum I would have had to swim was not more than two miles at a stretch. I was aware that many islands were very small and uninhabited, but they would have been good resting grounds.

On a lonely spot I had discarded my uniform and slipped into sea in my under-clothes. Tucked into my shorts were my savings ($30), wrapped in a cigarette packet's silver foil. Wading into the tepid water, I began to swim in a steady breaststroke. About a quarter of a mile out, I saw a splash some 50 yards away from me. A whitish-yellow shape glistened momentarily in the moonlight. Then in a flash I realised what it was. It had completely escaped my mind that the sea was shark infested! It took me no time to decide that it was a far more tolerable proposition to stay alive even in the prison camp than become a feast for the sharks. I had no difficulty in getting back to the shore, but could not find the spot where I had discarded my uniform. In my wet under-clothes, I very stealthily crept back to Farrer Park. I was back with 45 Army Troops Company before the first light on 17 February.

Colonel Bhonsle, who had assumed that I was on my way to India, appeared very disappointed on meeting me, only a few days later. When I told him why, he told me it was foolish of me to return. He was certain that I would now never get out of a prison camp. It is possible that he was annoyed that I could not convey his message to his wife.

We stayed in Farrer Park for two or three days. We saw the formal ceremony of the Indian Army personnel being handed over to the Japanese by a British officer. The Japanese in their language harangued us. We saw a few Indian officers moving freely almost as equals with the enemy.

True, the fall of Singapore must have come as a shock to the Allies. But I am sure that the Japanese were also very surprised at the thousands of prisoners they had on their hands. The task of accommodating us must have been gigantic. Committed, as they were to make capital of racial discrimination as propaganda, the problems were indeed acute for the Japanese.

As a first step, the Indian prisoners of war were split into groups to occupy the various military barracks all over Singapore. We were allotted the Bidadari Camp and the 45th Army Troops Company was again on the road towards Bidadari. As we trudged along, we were witness to the ghastly scenes of pillage and plunder that had ravaged the city. We passed through smoking rubble with knots of Chinese and Malay civilians looking at us with silent sympathy. Goods rejected by the satiated looters were scattered all over the streets. Among them were very many books, curios, golf clubs and the like.

I felt a tap on my shoulder. "Saheb, one of the men just picked these books up." One was a book titled *On The Run* and the other a large 'Phillips International Atlas for Naval Officers'. I clearly sensed the hand of providence in preparing me for an escape. These books were quickly dumped in the ration truck that was crawling in front of us. They became my constant companions for the next few months and were a great source of inspiration. Thus equipped, I entered my first Prison Camp.

2

CROSSING MALAYA

The sprawling Bidadari Camp looked nothing like a prison camp. It was a maze of timber huts with atap roofs (thatched roofing), built on undulating ground in barrack fashion to house the growing strength of garrison troops in Singapore after the outbreak of war in 1939. There were a number of Chinese cemeteries, a few permanent houses and excellent metalled roads within the camp. The camp was already becoming crowded, but as we had arrived fairly early, we were able to choose an area to our liking — secluded and detached. Close by was a large stack of crates, obviously the dumps of our supply depot.

Soon, the Japanese came and got busy. A soldier stood sentry at the roadside next to the row of boxes and away from our barracks. It was obvious that he did not expect any marauders from within the camp, but was to watch against any civilian approaching the dumps. Despite the ever-present sentry, we soon found out that the cases contained tinned food. In a matter of a few nights, the dumped goods became considerably smaller in size. The tinned food was quickly distributed, and hidden away to be rationed later. Similarly, some petrol drums were quickly rolled away and camouflaged in a deep drain. These stocks came in very useful in running our battery charging sets, and later, in keeping some of the officers mobile.

The Japanese war booty was beyond all dreams of the avaricious. They must have been staggered at the vast quantity of motor vehicles, both army and civilian. The storage of these vehicles did not present any serious problems. They spent a few days driving chains of them through the streets and dumping them in any open space available. Our Bren-carriers were used the most to tow the chains, each of which comprised as many as seven or eight vehicles in tow.

Suddenly a vast dump of assorted vehicles grew near our barracks. A very enterprising officer from our lot began working on this pile and almost in no time had a small staff car ready to go on road. Considerable thought was given to the matter of parking. It had to be where the approach was difficult, but driving in and out from the dump easy.

In the beginning, this vehicle was driven about stealthily within our camp area, just to relieve the boredom of the POWs. During the same period, we found an Australian 5-ton truck regularly being parked overnight next to our barrack. This vehicle was regularly driven out of the camp early in the morning, returning after dark. The driver was invariably a Japanese soldier. The distinction marking to indicate that this vehicle was on Japanese Army duty was, merely a piece of paper, stuck on the windscreen with certain Japanese lettering. One night, this piece of paper was peeled off and pasted on to the windscreen of our little vehicle.

The next step was rather a bold one. Four of us got into the car and drove up to the Japanese sentry at the main gate. If challenged, we were to leave the car and scamper right back into the camp. But, much to our surprise, the sentry found nothing suspicious and happily waved us out of the camp. After a short run on the open streets of Singapore, we returned to the camp. We had no plans to escape. While getting out of prison camp was thus made easy, getting out of Singapore Island was fraught with danger. Knowing this, the guards could afford to be slack.

These outings in the staff car brightened up our gloomy life to some extent. Ours was the only barrack with electricity, thanks to a sentry who allowed us to tap power from the mains close by. Each one of us had a bedside lamp, and were one of the very few to have our night meals at a sensible time. The rest of the camp had to finish their dinner before darkness set in.

All these days, the ring round the camp had been closing in. Prisoners were allotted stretches of the perimeter to dig and the spill over on the inner side of the camp to be used to build an embankment. Barbed wire fencing came up and soon all irregular movement in and out of the prison camp came to a stop.

However, thousands of troops went out daily on fatigue duties, leaving by first light and returning after darkness had set in. Officers had to take their turn as commanders of this labour force. During such 'outings' I talked to many civilians, though only surreptitiously. I was left in no doubt that conditions were worse outside the camp.

Even when ration scarcity set in and most food items had

completely run out, we continued to get two *chappathis* (Indian bread) a day. And there was tea, but no sugar and milk. One just got used to it soon enough.

What troubled some of us, more than the physical hardship, was the mental strain. The first pathetic scene occurred within a few days of our entering Bidadari. The perimeter defence had not taken shape. A miserable looking creature, a young man of some 25 years, was begging my men for some food. They curtly told him that our rations were very meager. I talked to him and found out he was a Maratha gunner taken prisoner in Hong Kong. He had escaped, and made a perilous and arduous journey to Singapore, believing it would be in British hands. He entered the island a few days after ceasefire and had been starving for a long time.

I was amazed at the achievement of this semi-literate luckless individual. I pointed out to him that if he had taken only a half right turn earlier on in his travel, he would have been in safe hands. His answer was matter of fact. He was an ignorant soldier, who knew nothing of geography. He had reached the limit of his endurance. If we did not assist him, he said, he had no alternative but to go to the streets and die. I had no difficulty in convincing my men that this gunner would henceforth remain with our unit.

Among the Indian troops, health and morale was low, and bickering on the increase. As our rations depleted, tempers grew short. A Subedar (Junior Commissioned Officer), suspected of distributing food unfairly, was beaten to death by other prisoners. In another case, a depressed army doctor took his own life. Ganpat Shinde, one of my sappers, came to me one day with a strange request — I was to send him to India! Though I tried to reason with him on that occasion, it was clear he had become insane. He would sit all day in front of my barrack continuously muttering "*Saheb mujhe ghar bhejdo*" (Sir, please send me home). I could do nothing but feel sorry for him.

These incidents and many others began to prey on my mind. But it was not just this ugly and pathetic fact of prison camp life that strengthened my determination to get away. Far more important, oddly enough, was a jocular remark made in Kirkee nearly a year earlier. I was being posted overseas and in the regimental mess one evening, some officers were teasing me about my being southerner who did not belong to the martial class. Our Chief Instructor, Major Swinhoe, joined us. "Yes, Pillai," he said with a smile, "now that you are off to war, I hope you won't let us down". He was joking, but his words had rankled in my mind ever since. Was it not a POW's duty to escape, if it was feasible? Well, this POW was not going to shirk his duty!

I had by then finished reading many of those escape stories. Often I kept staring at the Atlas, longingly looking at the map of India and despairing over the vast expanse of water that came between my homeland and me.

I was determined to get out, but once out, where could I go? Singapore was surrounded on three sides by the sea. Getting a boat was impossible, and I was not going to enter those shark-infested waters again. The land route was therefore the only option. This meant that my journey would have to be long and over unknown territory. Sumatra had fallen to the Japanese days before. I was very vague indeed in my mind whether I should head for Chungking (in China) or Burma. I thought of my acquaintance and was anxious to contact him. Enos, my wine waiter in the mess proved to be the answer. Now free from serving in the mess, he was anxious to become a civilian and set up a small business. I gave him $10 and the permission to slip away while out on fatigue duties. In return, he was to contact Radhakrishnan and convey the message that I was well and very anxious to meet him.

Enos met me again years later in India. He certainly remained faithful to his promise. He did convey my message to Radhakrishnan who visited me early in April 1941. He informed me that an Indian was free to move about in Singapore if he possessed a membership card of the Indian Independence League, a newly formed association. He also said that it was easy to obtain this card on payment of a nominal fee. No awkward questions were asked. I requested Radhakrishnan to get me a card. It occurred to me that a new identity would be an added safety factor. I gave the name that first came into my head. After some ten days, I was in possession of a membership card vouching for the patriotic credentials of one KS Ramachandran.

I had taken Radhakrishnan into confidence. He showed willingness to throw in his lot with mine, but wanted some assurance that we would reach India safely. He needed some time to think it over, before taking a final decision.

The Atlas equipped me with a fund of information I could not have done without. I learnt the names of all the mountain passes between India and Burma. I found out how dense the jungles were and how high the hilly regions between China and India, or Burma and Siam were. All I had to do was repeatedly compare the tone of the colouring on the maps with similar features on areas already familiar to me.

I thought a string of names on the likely routes might be of some use and I was soon very busy memorising a few series. Methods advocated by the Pelmanism booklets, brought quick results in these attempts. It was obvious that no matter the route, vast distances would have to be covered on foot. My service boots, already showing signs of wear, were certainly inadequate for the task. Even a brand new pair of tough boots would be torn to shreds in such terrain. Another danger was they would draw the attention of the enemy. Everything pointed to a long bare foot trek ahead for me.

I was soon learning the feel of bare feet on rough ground by walking all around the camp for as long as possible. It was tough going, but gradually both my mind and feet grew tough to the extent that I stopped feeling any soreness or inconvenience, as long as I did not step on ragged stones or a thorn. Preoccupied by these toughening and memory exercises, I ignored and was ignored by my colleagues at first. Little surprise that some of them thought I was touched in the head. Their opinion did not bother me till I saw one of them gesturing to another that I had gone over the bend. This incident disturbed me no end, because I started to wonder if, indeed, I had not gone slightly mad because of the stress and strain of the last several months.

Initially, I had planned to escape alone, but gradually I came to the conclusion that I should have a companion. I strongly felt I would need human companionship, specially since the Atlas was reminding me constantly of the vast distance I would have to cover. It also became clear to me that medicine was an absolute necessity in a journey of this magnitude. Having been a victim of malaria even on my way out from India, and considering the dense jungles that were in the region, I started collecting Atebrin tablets from various medical officers in the camp. It occurred to me that an ideal companion would be a person with some kind of medical training on this perilous journey.

One naturally hesitates in confiding to strangers, particularly in a prison camp. I went about sending very discreet feelers. One Captain Paul, of the Indian Medical Service (IMS), seemed to consider the mention of escape to India so ridiculous that I had to laugh it off as a joke. There was, however, another medical officer, a Captain Natarajan, whose mind had been working on the same lines as mine. I was soon convinced of his bonafides as well as his determination to get out. Natarajan, in many ways was a good choice. He too, was a Tamilian, and at 39, eight years older than me. As a doctor, he had access to the medical supplies and could easily build-up a cache of anti-malaria pills. Natarajan and I together had around $100, far too little for the long journey ahead. Reluctant to borrow money from other POWs, I thought of the only civilian in Singapore — K. Radhakrishnan. He had about $500, which he agreed to donate provided he could join us. He had sent his wife and two children to India before the war, and was anxious to rejoin them. Before long the three of us — Radhakrishnan, Natarajan and I — met at Bidadari and discussed the matter.

Radhakrishnan brought us encouraging news. Railway communications with the mainland had been restored and some civilians were being allowed to travel out of Singapore.

Natarajan promised to bring in a large stock of Atebrin pills, and Radhakrishnan was to secure a membership card of the Indian Independence League for our medical accomplice.

After the good news came the bad news. I was transferred along with other sapper units to Tyresall Camp, which housed what remained of a military hospital after the fire during the siege. I was lucky enough to be made Assistant Provost Marshal (APM) of this new camp, entrusted with the specific task of checking large scale desertions that were by then taking place from all prison camps. The Japanese were getting very perturbed over this factor. This onerous responsibility weighed heavily on me. There was, however, one advantage in my new assignment. I was free to go out of the camp, which enabled me to keep in touch with Natarajan.

On 6 May 1942, I was one of the many detailed to visit Bidadari, where I met Natarajan and discussed when we should escape. While there, I received a message that I had been detailed by name to listen on the following day to a lecture on the advantages of following the Rising Sun, the Japanese emblem. I thought the time had come for me to slip off.

I had earlier taken two or three of my friends partly into confidence. I was anxious to obtain a respite of some four days, which I considered adequate for me to get out of Malaya. When I told these friends that I was slipping out the same day, they were very worried. My Camp Commandant, one of the friends, pointed out that in view of next day's lecture, he could not keep my absence a secret. He wanted me to wait for another suitable opportunity. Finding me determined the others prevailed upon the Commandant and convinced him that he should cover my absence as long as his own safety allowed him. These friends gave me a farewell party as well as it could get. We drank from tea mugs sweetened with candy syrup and they proposed a toast for my safe journey. Their good wishes must have gone a long way indeed and I shall remember that parting as long as I shall live.

Natarajan met me at the appointed place on 6th May, and both of us were soon out of Bidadari. At 9 p.m. on May 06, we had dressed up in typical South-Indian clothes, a white shirt and dhoti. Nobody saw or challenged us, but in the train to Radhakrishnan's house my nerves were taut. I kept imagining that all other passengers were staring at us knowingly. We had timed our departure close to sunset, and therefore we had no difficulty in reaching Radhakrishnan's house. After dinner we spent a lot of time discussing our journey towards the mainland of Malaya and the possible risks we might be running in the attempt. We decided that the best course was to lie low for a while, as the Japanese would be on the look out for us at all the exit points from Singapore. Two days later, we three went to the railway station at about sunset and bought three tickets for Perai, as we had decided to get as far away as possible from Singapore, and Penang was the only big town that came to our mind. We had obtained information regarding entry into Siam (Thailand) and Penang, as they suited our plans best. It was not a passenger train; all travelers had the choice of either travelling in the closed goods wagons or staying behind on the island. We were not fussy.

We detrained at Perai some two days later and made our way with the rest of the crowd towards the ferry for Penang. As we

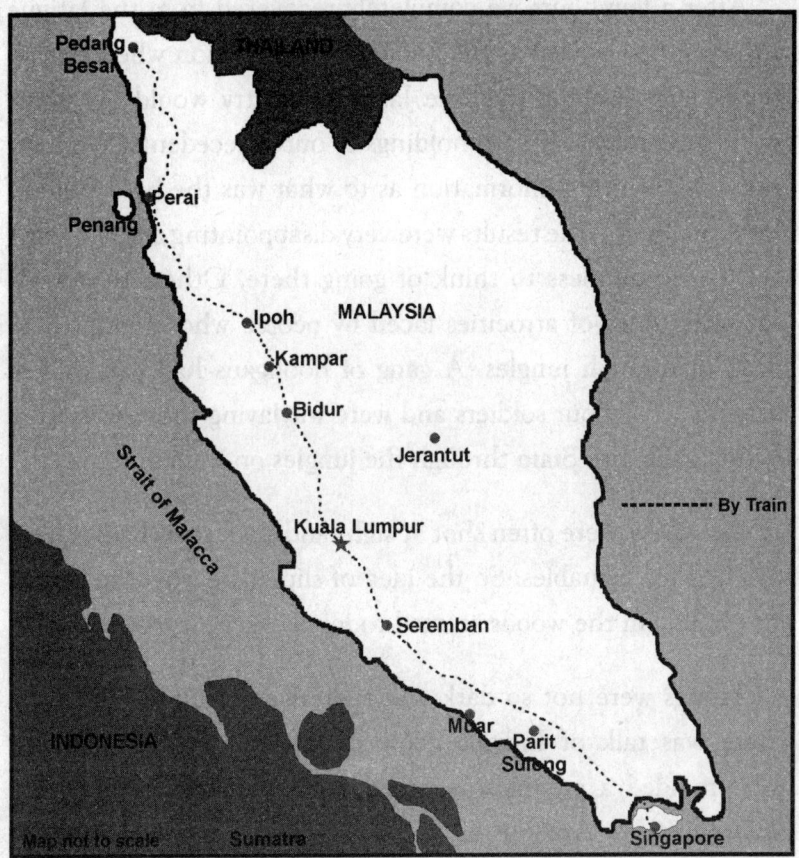

Fig. 2.1 Escape Through Malaya

neared the barrier, we had to make quite an effort to conceal our fear. After a cursory glance at our membership cards, the Japanese soldier on duty waved us forward. We paid a very small amount for the crossing and landed safely in Penang.

We three were clear in our minds that we had to look and act as what our aliases claimed we were. We took a room in a South Indian Brahmin hotel. The food was tasty, accommodation adequate and charges very moderate. We spent three days in Penang.

After a few hours we completely recovered from the fatigue of the journey as well as the nerve-racking tension when getting off the ferry, hoping that the Japanese sentry would not show undue interest in our cash holdings or our antecedents. We soon got busy collecting information as to what was the best route of entry into Siam. The results were very disappointing at first. Some said it was madness to think of going there. Others recounted harrowing tales of atrocities faced by people who attempted to sneak in through jungles. A gang of hooligans had got hold of weapons left by our soldiers and were waylaying those who were trying to slip into Siam through the jungles on the border.

Travellers were often shot at sight and then their bodies were searched for valuables. So the idea of slipping across the border after hiding in the woods seemed to involve serious risks.

Things were not so dark and there was a glimmer of hope. There was talk of Indians being permitted to enter Siam by rail, provided a permit was issued to that effect by the Army of Occupation. Anxious as I was to avoid getting close to the Japanese, contacting them was necessary. We needed to know exactly how the system worked for getting the permits. The application forms had to be filled in with the usual particulars of names of applicant and his father, age, address and so on. The snag was that two photographs of passport size must be attached. Radhakrishnan's photos were not a problem, but for the remaining two of us, photographs would be a sure give away.

Eventually we saw there was no option but to attach the snaps, whatever the consequences. But anxious to minimize the risk of detection, we decided to dim the lighting of the photographs.

We also had to ensure that they would acquire a faded look in a month or so. We finally contacted a Chinese photographer with known anti-Japanese sentiments. Whether he believed our half true explanations or not, we'll never know. What mattered was that he gave each of us two copies of our photographs with the assurance that the faces on them would become unrecognizable in 30 days.

Next morning, the three of us stood nervously before the Japanese officers at the headquaters. We told them that we were traders. "What trade?" one officer barked "Potatoes and onions" replied Radhakrishnan promptly. He added: "We want to import from Thailand and sell to the Japanese army here". Natarajan and I were getting our answers ready but there was no need. The officer smiled and gave us the permits. In a short time we left the Japanese headquarters armed with passports. We were calling each other by the fictitious names on our papers to get used to it. My name was K.S. Ramachandran, the name I had assumed on 6th May.

As it was late in the afternoon, we spent the night in Penang and entered the ferry the following morning. We then took a train to Padang Besar, arriving at the frontier railway post on the Siamese border by noon the same day. There were no trains beyond Padang Besar. Within a short period of our detraining, the station was deserted, except for a handful of railway staff. There was also a Japanese contingent with an officer-in-charge, who was strolling on the platform. A passenger train came in. We waited for the officer and his men to get on, but they did not and nor could we. With heavy hearts we watched the train steam off.

There were only few passengers on the train. Passports we got at such risk proved of no use. We could not understand why.

When the last train on that day left, we began to feel the pangs of hunger. We had not thought of food because we had been sure we would be on a train soon. Padang Besar was a small station and practically deserted by even the staff after the departure of the last train. Only the Japanese soldiers were on the premises besides us. We spent a despondent night at the station. We soon began to panic. Were the details on our passports being scrutinized again? The Japanese officer was constantly busy at the telephone. But then, he had hardly glanced at our passports. We were in a quandary.

The dawn and the hustle and bustle around us somewhat lifted our gloom. We repeated our entreaties to the Japanese, but he kept shrugging us off and once, in a fit of temper, chased us out of the platform. About midday a train with a load of timber flats came in and was waiting to steam off to Siam. The official finally relented and waved us towards the train just as it was pulling out. We made a dash and clambered on to the flats. Life was not so bad, after all! The Siamese were using paddy husks as fuel for the locomotive, and it was belching embers that were showering down on us. But we were too elated to care. The countryside was lovely, but no more so than on the Malayan side of the border. But to our eyes it started to look lovelier and lovelier as our feeling of safety increased.

3

THROUGH SIAM

Hat Yai station was in sight. The train had slowed down, as the signal was red. One could have safely got out of the train and walked off. We never thought of doing that. Were we not armed with permits to enter Siam. As no passengers were expected to be on this train the Hat Yai Junction wore a deserted look. Immediately on alighting, however, two serious looking gentlemen confronted us. We showed them our papers, but they meant nothing to these men. It then dawned on us that they were emigration officials. A tall uniformed Siamese bore down on us. "Your papers", he demanded. We handed them over. His face darkened. "You don't have visas for Siam," he said. "Come with me."

We three were illegal immigrants into Siam and we would have to spend that night in a jail and stay there till we came up for trial. This was indeed terrible news. As we were being marched off from the station, a passer-by, an Indian, took notice of us and inquired what was wrong. "My name is Sundaram Pillai," he said, scribbling his address on piece of paper and added "come over when you have finished." He seemed to have influence over the local officials. He was a Tamilian, domiciled in Siam and married to a local girl. He expressed his sympathy and gave us directions to his residence, which was close by and then went on his way.

Our escorts took us to an office building, noted down our particulars and took our thumbprints. It soon became clear that the Thai immigration official had no intention of giving us our visas. In fact, he threatened to deport us back to Malaya the next morning. Then remembering the Indian who had just met us, I asked the official, if we could contact him. He thought it over. Pointing to Radhakrishnan, he said: "You go". Radhakrishnan was soon out to contact our sympathiser en-route. He found Sundaram Pillai and, after some persuasion and financial temptation, he agreed to bail us out. By sunset, we were free men again with an official permit from Siamese authorities this time. The contents of the permit were not translated to us but under the circumstances, we were in no mood to worry.

We spent that night under the hospitable roof of Sundaram Pillai. He gave us a nice dinner and soon we were engrossed in discussing the business aspect of the assistance. Radhakrishnan had promised him a substantial sum of money in return for his rescue services and was expecting some $600. This might have been due to Radhakrishnan's reference during earlier meetings that we had $600.

Between the three of us, we did have a little over $600 at this stage. But then we were still a long way from our homes. Sundaram Pillai was satisfied with $450. This was a crushing blow. Three quarters of our money gone — and we had been travelling for barely a week! "Start tightening your belt," I muttered to Radhakrishnan, who had begun to develop cold feet. We came to know that Pillai had stood bail for us against the emigration official's advice. The latter seemed to have been of the firm opinion that we three were communist agents and were probably going to incite some trouble in his country. Our benefactor warned his wife and children's safety depended very much on our conduct in Siam. Our stay was only for 30 days and he beseeched us to return to Malaya within that period. We gave him a solemn pledge that we would leave the country before that. He appeared to be unaware of the slight difference between his demand and our promise and was quite satisfied.

During all these discussions, there were a number of visits by his wife into that room. She never spoke a word, but merely kept looking at us with pathos and bewilderment on her face. She must have felt some bad omens for her family. I am very happy to say the three of us escapees behaved in an impeccable manner during our stay in her country, never crossed the path of the law and left the country well before the stipulated period. I am fairly certain that the Sundaram Pillais' were spared any inconvenience on our account. I sincerely hoped so, at any rate.

That night, we ate well. Mrs Pillai, a petite Siamese, was silent throughout the meal, but our host was in an expansive mood. On learning that we were traders headed for Bangkok, he suggested that we first go to Trang, 100 miles from HatYai, where he had a good friend, Valliapa Chettiar, a money lender. "This man knows all the businessmen in Bangkok," Pillai said. The next move was to promptly arrive at HatYai railway station the next morning. Our destination was Trang. There was a slight snag in getting tickets. We were refused at first and soon found the reason. We three were clad in South Indian clothes with a small cloth bag hung over our shoulder containing our change of clothing. A person next door, though a Siamese, realised our plight and came to our rescue. He gave us three tickets for Trang and the balance of our money.

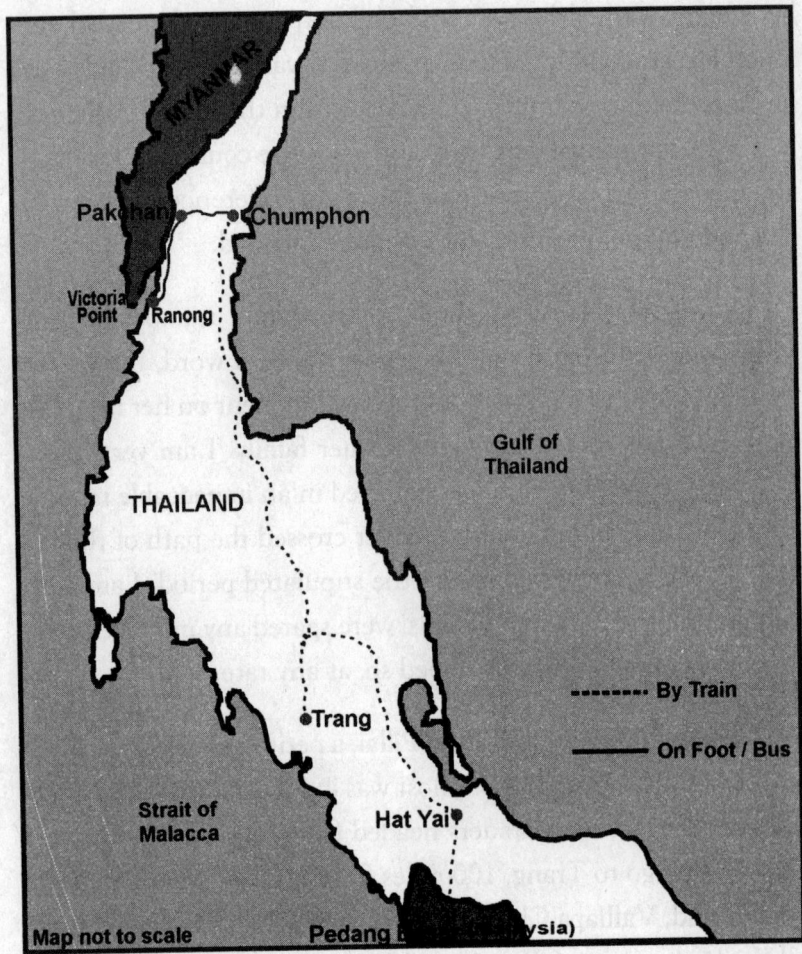

Fig. 3.1 Escape Through Siam (Thailand)

Siam left three lasting impressions on my mind. The first was the diminutive size of the women. Several times I saw groups of school aged girls walking ahead of me, but when they turned around, they turned out to be full grown women in the prime of their lives. The next remarkable feature was that though most of the women folk went about wearing frocks and attractive hats, they were inevitably barefooted. I was informed that these were not rich women. They could hardly afford the clothes and the hats they wore. So they drew the line at footwear and trod the land barefort. I was amused, but then that's how the world is.

But what left the deepest impression on my mind was the remarkable politeness of the Siamese people. Of the many instances, I need to recount only one. During one of our rail journeys, I was sitting alone by the window in a third class compartment. A Siamese soldier in uniform got on to find that every seat was occupied except the one next to me. I saw him come in, but anxious to maintain distance from all soldiers, whether Japanese or Siamese, I kept my eyes on the scenery outside. After a while, seeing him still standing in the passage holding his pack I merely pointed out the vacant space beside me. He sat down with a bow and kept the pack between us on the bench. I was not frightened of looking at him, as he had picked up a small book and was reading intently. After quite some time, he opened his pack and took out something to eat. He offered the container to me and insisted on my partaking his fare. I was indeed very touched at this high degree of politeness. I was not hungry at that time, but I did not wish my refusal to smell of any bias, thereby offending him.

We reached Trang without any difficulty. We found a number of Indians, mostly Sikhs. We left our belongings in a cheap hotel and started making enquiries about South Indians in general. Valliappa Chettiar and Narayanan Chettiar were the two moneylenders in that town.

While passports and permits were adequate to meet the questions of the Siamese and Japanese, the Chettiars had no difficulty in seeing through our pretences. They instantly made out we were no businessmen by any stretch of imagination. If we three were to make any headway in obtaining even small assistance from them, we needed to win their trust. We pretended to disclose our real identity after considerable hedging. We maintained that I was a school-teacher, in Seremban, Radhakrishnan what he really was, and Natarajan as a new arrival in Malaya. These claims convinced them. Yet the only assistance we could get from these money lenders was the advice that it would be better for us to stick it out in Malaya or Siam till the war ended. They maintained that Phuket Island would be a good refuge if we wanted to avoid the Japanese.

These suggestions did not fit in with our schemes. We tried to ascertain our prospects of entering China via Indo-China (Vietnam) or even direct from Siam (Thailand). They said the chances were very dim and most of the persons we consulted thought we must be out of our minds to take such risk. It never occurred to these people that at least two of us were real fugitives and that our very lives depended on reaching our native land or some place where the Allies still held sway.

This was the picture painted to us. Bangkok was full of Japanese and very few South Indians chose to stay on there. As one travelled further up north, all Indians would come under close scrutiny, particularly South Indians. Under the circumstances, we became even more determined to enter Indo-China and increase the distance from the point of our escape.

Not having had very rigid plans about our route, it was not difficult to think of another one with better prospects of getting us into China. Why could we not enter the safety zone direct from Siam? Chiangmai was a railway terminus nearest to the Chinese border and earlier on I had noticed in the Atlas that there was a good, winding road over hilly country; by this route, the Chinese border was less than 200 miles. The freedom with which we were moving around in Siam convinced us that our next destination had to be Chiangmai.

But our explorations showed us that skirting Bangkok to reach Chiangmai safely was very difficult. Being the only three South Indians in the area who could not speak a word of Siamese was in itself a high risk situation How I wished then that the time and effort I had put in earlier on to acquire a good knowledge of Malay had been devoted instead on Chinese. It might have been of some use to the party, but then again, may be not.

Further enquiries in Trang convinced us to not only abandon all hopes of getting into China, but also to forget the Burma route as an alternative. Everyone dissuaded us from this idea, saying that the only way to Burma was by the sea and there were no more coastal steamers plying.

It was stated, however, that one might be able to get to Victoria Point, really the land's end of Burma in the south. But though connected with the rest of Burma by land this little outpost was to all intents and purposes an island. Beyond this town were very thick jungles, high mountains and no habitation at all for some two to three hundred miles. I had gathered a similar impression from the map.

While in captivity, there were a few lectures, which the prisoners had to listen to. The main burden of these talks were to convince one and all that it would be futile for Indians to think of escaping via Burma. The area south of Mergui, could not be crossed by any human being and the terrain between Burma and India was covered with thick impenetrable jungles which abounded in wild animals and poisonous snakes. Such threatening references were not made about the terrain to China. This must have been why we had first opted for Chungking.

With China beyond our reach, Burma was the Hobsons choice. Despite the overwhelming evidence that work our way in that direction. Without appearing to be very keen, we collected a great deal of information regarding Ranong, a Siamese coastal town slap opposite Victoria Point and separated only by a small estuary barely two miles wide. Before the outbreak of war, one Narayanan Chettiar, a banker was doing business out of Ranong. The local reports at Trang were definite that the banker would have left for Bangkok if not for India. There would probably be only an employee taking care of the premises.

Despite all this discouragement, Ranong became our immediate objective. We bade goodbye to the two or three Tamilians and entrained for a place known as Chumphon, some 225 miles due North. We reached this town early one afternoon. As had become the usual procedure, we were on the look out for some Indian, preferably from the South, but with little success. We were not anxious to let anyone know we could speak English.

Even if we did so, one was not sure of being understood in the heart of Siam. In our wanderings that day we came across a South Indian, who was himself a stranger to that town. He could not help us much beyond advising us to take a bus journey to Pakchan due West from Chumphon, some 40 miles away. It seemed to be the right thing to do, for it was on the road leading to Ranong. He further advised us to stay in some hotel for the night. This was sound advice, as there were many Japanese soldiers even in this remote town. We three entered an establishment which looked like an eating place. After eating some kind of food, we accosted someone who was probably the proprietor and, more with gestures than words, tried to convey to him that we needed a room for the night. Eventually he understood, but he found the money we offered highly unattractive. Then followed a period of bargaining, in which he matched our anxiety with his patience. We kept on showing currencies of various denominations and concocted a system of communication in which each party had to signify the price quoted/accepted by touching the notes of suitable value. Finally, when he realised that what we offered was the total sum for all three and not individual payments, he was crestfallen, but he did not have the heart to turn us out. If he had, we would have been in a soup, because the police were regularly rounding up all loiterers in the night.

The proprietor did not give us a room, but waved us towards a passage in between two rows of rooms. We did not object. With the main gate for protection, we curled up on the corridor floor. We can safely say that this was the most memorable night for the two worst possible reasons. The first were the bed bugs. They swarmed over the entire corridor and all over us, quite immune to the dim light and biting into us any and everywhere without ever coming up for air. Nowhere on earth could there possibly have been a building with such a density of vermin population. Second, it quickly became clear that this hellhole was called an eating-place only as a cover. It was actually a brothel and a cheap one at that.

One has nightmares while one sleeps. What do you call it when a nightmare keeps you awake? Even the world of vermin seemed to conspire against us fugitives. When, out of sheer exhaustion, we almost managed to ignore these despicable creations of God, there were the tormentors in human form — the continuous comings and goings of nocturnal visitors to this "hole of ill fame". Many of them were drunk, and when they tripped over us in the dark, they expressed their annoyance in vehement tones, but in a language fortunately unintelligible to us. We dared not go beyond an occasional, inaudible mutter, lest it should end up in a brawl. So, the whole night we were violated, both in body and human dignity. Desperately, we awaited the dawn. Early in the morning we moved out to the pavement. As soon as we saw people moving about on the road we started our search for the transport terminus. There we had some biscuits and coffee for breakfast. Once on the bus carrying us to Pakchan through the winding mountain road, the terrible experience of the previous night receded far to the back of our minds. The feeling of being continually on the move towards freedom gave us a sense of purpose and satisfaction.

Halting for a short while at Pakchan the bus headed west towards Ranong. We were speedily climbing down, but there were a number of long halts. At one of the stops we espied a stretch of water hardly half a mile wide. Burma was on the other side. The thought of swimming across was almost irresistible. A brief discussion was enough to dismiss the idea. Natarajan and I were good swimmers, but for the first time we learnt that

Radhakrishnan could not swim a stroke. He was generous enough to suggest that he could make his way to Ranong alone and we could swim across if we so desired. We decided to stick together.

Radhakrishnan was a sensitive and impulsive person. He began blaming himself for our lost opportunity and imagining that our disappointment was greater than it really was. Natarajan and I would certainly have been put to death if we were caught by the Japanese. Radhakrishnan did not run such a risk. But the fear of being caught was far from our minds and that is why we were not overly disappointed that our companion could not swim.

Alighting at Ranong, we three walked slowly up a street, which turned out to be the main road. The first person to greet us was a man from the West coast of India, whose name was Abu Bakr. I think he was doing some business in Siam. We never quite found out, but he was a man of considerable importance in the locality. The Siamese held him in high esteem and the local Japanese consul was said to be very envious of the foreigner's prestige. Abu Bakr himself treated the Japanese consul with the greatest of contempt, probably understandable under the circumstances. This high dignitary seemed to have been only a common photographer in Ranong, but the Japanese successes had placed him on a high pedestal.

Abu Bakr was a rough diamond, a person of strong likes and dislikes, yet with sterling qualities. He took charge of us almost immediately. Our first query was about the whereabouts of Narayanan Chettiar, a banker whose name we were told in Trang. He had left Ranong for Bangkok and was not likely to return for some time. We had no hesitation, therefore, in claming acquaintance with him and deeply regretting his absence. Abu Bakr gave us a lot of encouragement and promises and help to the best of his ability. He secured us some cheap lodgings, introduced us to another friend of his who was running a tea stall.

Within a couple of days we came to know all the Indians there, comprising less than six families. Unrestricted movement throughout the streets of the town was a very welcome change. Most of our time was spent in collecting information about Burmese towns we were interested in — Mergui, Tavoy and Victoria Point, within a few miles from Ranong.

It was soon clear that even during peace Indian residents here had not bothered to know much about areas north of Mergui. Therefore, it was safe to lie to them that our relatives resided in the region of Moulmein.

Our funds were running low. If only Abu Bakr had been told the truth about our financial conditions, no doubt he would have saved us the money we spent on our boarding. He thought that money was no problem to us. We dared not disillusion him, for he would then have wondered why, if we were so broke, we should concern ourselves with our kith and kin across the border.

We tuned in regularly to BBC and All India Radio. Their broadcasts, which claimed that the Japanese menace was under control, heartened Indians even in the remotest corner the world. We too hoped and prayed for a quick end to the war.

It was well known that the Japanese Consul in this town had three wives and was so partial to the second that he ate out of her hands. This talented Siamese lady was said to be sympathetic to Indians. The Consular residence had no guards or protection and was easily accessible to one and all, like any other house in town. We three had tried jointly and individually to plead with Japanese officials for permits, but to no avail.

I had worn my most dejected look to win the sympathy of this kindly lady. She listened to us patiently. Then hoping to ingratiate ourselves further, I asked if I could do any chores around her home. She led me to the kitchen and I spent the next couple of hours grinding masalas (spices). I must have managed to win her over, for she exerted her influence on her husband for us, the three wretched Indians. The 'great man' relented and granted us permits to enter Victoria Point. Why should he not? We were, after all, three loyal subjects of the Imperial Majesty of Japan, who were merely attempting to get in touch with their relatives in Burma. We had stuck to this story throughout our stay.

Our experience in Padang Besar had not been forgotten. The commander at that Frontier railway station in Malaya had virtually repudiated the passes issued by a formation headquarter at Penang. But the situation was different here and the Consul was the sole power for the time being. We were not wrong in our assumptions.

The next step was to intimate the Siamese emigration authorities of the area that their country would soon be rid of us. We were anxious to ensure that our benefactor at HatYai did not come to any harm on our account. We had been in Siam for about 20 days, well under the stipulated period. I am sure the Siamese official would have passed on the necessary information to appropriate authorities. Detailed entries were made on an impressive looking official document and endorsed. We already had the visas.

For the last time, we walked along the main road of the town and arrived at the site of the ferry. There was a small boat with oars, ready to convey the daily cargo of vegetables and other commodities to Victoria Point. We paid, got on the boat and were swiftly rowed across this stretch of water. A Japanese sentry was silhouetted against the horizon of the far shore. We just couldn't be bothered.

4

THE BURMA GRIND

TO RANGOON

On reaching Victoria Point one of the boatmen alighted and walked past the sentry, while the second moored his craft. When we three also tried to walk past him casually, the man grunted. We abruptly stopped where we were, acting scared, which was the normal thing to do, but we did not let him sence the real fear we felt. The sentry's face was utterly expressionless. He took a long time scrutinizing our papers. He saw our membership cards for the Indian Independence League. This was in English. He cursorily glanced at the visas, which were presumably in Siamese. He carefully studied the other two sets of documents issued by his countrymen at Penang and Ranong. Even if he had known all the three languages and had read each piece of paper, he need not have taken such a long time. The second boatman also went past us at this stage. The sentry merely nodded to him. Obviously, the boatmen were regulars. I felt this was turning out to be a very long moment of truth, of life or death. But we needn't have worried. He returned our papers and waved us off towards Victoria Point.

The sentry was probably looking for a little diversion from the monotony of his duties. But it might have been equally true that he was suspicious of the three strange Indians who had come all the way from Singapore. He might have been looking for some expression on our face to confirm his doubts. Throughout his investigations, he did not speak a word. But we kept repeating two 'magic words' to convince him of our bona fides. Every time we caught him looking at one of us, comparing us with our photographs we chanted: 'India, Gandhi' — the words which were frequently used between Japanese and Indians.

Allowed to proceed with the papers in our hands, we found it almost impossible to resist our desire to scream in sheer relief. To appear normal, we busied ourselves sorting out the precious papers just within a few yards of the sentry. We kept jabbering for a minute or two in Tamil to lend verity to our acting.

We then climbed with steady, confident steps the steep path to Victoria Point. This frontier outpost was indeed a very small place. There was one narrow street with houses and shops on both sides of it.

One store was much bigger than all the rest and we entered its premises and parked ourselves on a bench in the verandah. We had come to the correct place. The proprietor of this store was one Lamba Kaka, about whom Abu Bakr had spoken of very highly.

He greeted us very cordially, asked us a few relevant questions, such as, where we came from and whether we had a comfortable journey and so on. Without even waiting for our answers in full, he went inside. It was soon clear that his disappearance was merely to provide us with some hot tea and biscuits. We spent the remainder of the day sitting there, and watching the movements of people on the street and the remarkable manner in which Lamba Kaka was carrying on his business.

We saw many Indians, practically no Burmese, and a small garrison of Japanese troops. There were also one or two white men — Australian prisoners of war from Malaya.

Our host, a Moplah from the west coast of India, had been given his nickname because he was tall and thin. What his real name was I never found out. In the few days of our stay here we saw some incidents which were remarkable, to say the least. Whoever he was and whatever he did before the war, he was now a changed man, and making money was certainly not what motivated this towering figure.

The Japanese garrison was guarding a bunch of Australian prisoners, forced to labour at some important war project somewhere near Victoria Point. During rest period, the guards allowed a few of these miserable POWs to roam a while on the only street, hoping to get some food. Many of them came to Lamba Kaka's establishment often singly and occasionally in groups, not exceeding three in number. Lamba Kaka's kindness to them needed to be seen to be believed. He handed out the goods, accepting whatever money was offered to him. Kaka never missed espying any penniless Aussie looking longingly at some tinned foodstuff. He would quickly collect a few tins of fish, cheese, butter or anything edible that was handy and thrust them into the pockets of the dumbfounded prisoner.

The stories of his generosity travelled like wild fire among the prisoners. I saw many an Australian enter the shop and come out carrying an abundance of food items far beyond his means. Some of them were too overcome with gratitude to express it in words. There was no need. Their eloquent eyes said every thing better than words ever could.

Lamba Kaka's open-handed charity was unsullied by ostentation or any other selfish motives. His general store must have been a source of steady income earlier. I did not find out how long he had been in business, nor could I assess the extent of his wealth. But the transactions he carried out during the few days that I was there would certainly have made serious inroads into his reserves. With the cessation of all mercantile shipping in these waters, his turnover must have dropped down to a trickle — the little that could come from the interior of Siam via Ranong.

I never could find out what motivated this Moplah to become Victoria Point's fountainhead of charity. All I could think of was that Nature had infused in him a sense of unassailable optimism and unparalleled kindness. He had no thought for his immediate safety, let alone the distant future. I sincerely hope that no harm ever came to him and that he was able to regain the wealth he had fed to the river of charity.

I got the chance to talk freely with the Australians many times and compared notes about their camp here and mine in Singapore. They had been in captivity only for a few months, but that is all it takes for depression to set in. One or two of them did manage to smile occasionally.

The Japanese guards were a mixed lot, attitude wise. There were many who had no hesitation in allowing a prisoner to stay out of the camp for quite a length of time. They were certainly taking no risks, as no prisoner in his senses could ever have even thought of attempting a getaway by land. The sea was virtually closed to them.

There were some guards, who augmented their pocket money by charging a premium from a prisoner who wanted to go outside the camp. There was one who was either a sadistic brute or just plain, mean sub-human. One such bad apple was enough. His modus operandi was simplicity itself. He would pocket the money and let the prisoners go out, but when they returned, he would order them to strip and coolly take possession of all the articles of food.

There was a silver lining to the cloud for the hapless Aussies. One of them was full of praise for a particular sentry, a very soft-hearted soldier indeed. He made it a habit to pass edible tit-bits to any prisoner who happened to be around. He went by the grand name of 'Sucker', a moniker concocted by some comedian among the inmates of the Prison Camp. But it was not meant to be derogatory. It was a typical Australian soldiers' way of expressing regard and gratitude without getting too mushy about it. For Lamba Kaka, it was in the natural course of things that we enjoyed his hospitality — food, shelter and good cheer — specially since we were acquainted with a man he truly admired, Abu Bakr.

Gradually my fear of being identified and captured receded. Of course one could never rule out such a possibility, but there was no real danger in this far off settlement, which was of little interest to the Japanese north of Rangoon. It was therefore very difficult to counter Kaka's advice to stay as his guests for the duration of the war. He insisted that he badly needed clerks who knew English and could easily use the three of us. We knew he was just trying to make us feel that we would not be living on charity.

We went on short walks ostensibly for exercising our limbs. We three took these excursions both together and separately. The aim was to explore the countryside to see if we could cross the Tenasserin Range and reach more populated areas of southern Burma. Mergui, the nearest town of some importance, was some miles up north. The area in between, we learnt, was mountainous, and wooded and with practically no human habitation. Yet, this appeared to be the only way out, as the monsoon was near and the fishermen, plying boats to Mergui had suspended their activities for some months.

Our restlessness and increasing anxiety did not escape the notice of our host. For a man of such deep compassion, our depression was contagious.

Lest he should think we were ungrateful to him, one day when I was alone I took him into my confidence. I told him a fair amount of truth about myself and some untruths about my two companions. It was the first time that I admitted to anyone that I was an escaped prisoner of war. It was not very difficult to convince my host that our continued stay in one place in such close proximity of the Japanese and within easy reach of Siam was fraught with danger. Also, by then, practically everyone knew that we three had come from Malaya. But I made Kaka believe in the lie that I was the only escapee from prison, the other two were civilians and that they knew nothing about my past. I believe he saw the urgency of our need to lose ourselves in some area in Burma where there would be a lot of Tamilians.

Our finances were at an all time low, even though living here did not cost us an anna. Had Lamba Kaka known our financial state I have no doubt in my mind that he would have been a river of generosity, but we didn't let him know. Reports assured us that there were many Tamilians from our home districts at Mergui and Tavoy and we hoped that someone would come to our assistance.

Kaka by now was convinced that our determination to keep on moving was quite natural. News reached us that some fishermen had planned to take one boat to Mergui despite the monsoon. I could not help thinking that our excellent host must have had much to do with this unexpected burst of courage on the part of the brave fishermen.

The journey by sea took more than just a few days. There were many halts, some times at an island and occasionally along the main coast. Always, land was within sight. I was not concerned very much about our safety. Natarajan appeared to be equally indifferent. But Radhakrishnan was, quite naturally, tense all through. For a non-swimmer was doomed to a watery grave if the boat capsized. The passengers and crew alike maintained silence most of the time, each obviously preoccupied with his own thoughts.

We noticed the apprehension, much to our concern, everytime they moored the boat at an island or the mainland. We realised

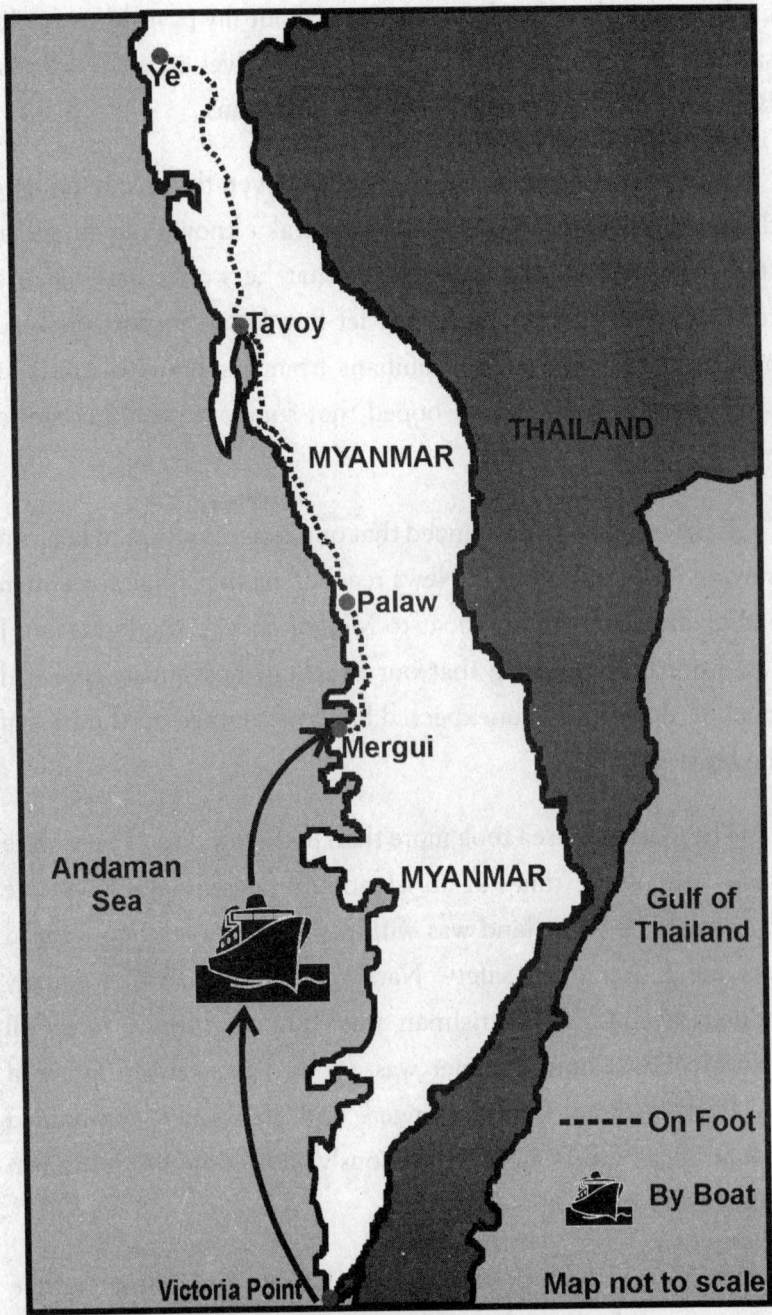

Fig: 4.1 Escape Through Burma (Myanmar)

that they were afraid of being attacked by some wild tribes. We all tensed up every time we halted. Radhakrishnan, of course took a sigh of relief whenever we touched land. Terra firma was his element, after all. But we two swimmers waited impatiently to be afloat again lest some wild tribals set upon us. On one occasion, the boatmen were just about to moor along the mainland when they suddenly changed their mind, swiftly put up sails and pushed away from the coast. We were close enough to the land to see three short, savage men — much like the Sakai tribesmen in the Paihang jungles of Malaya.

Mergui came within sight at last. It was almost midday. We saw many other boats anchored near the town. Our anxious glances saw only a few men moving about on the shore. Here again a Japanese sentry was standing on high ground near what appeared to be the landing jetty. Alarmed, we three had a hurried discussion. We comforted ourselves with the thought that the posting of this sentry had nothing to do with the arrival of two escaped prisoners of war and their companion, especially on an unexpected coastal sailing boat.

Convinced that there was no trap awaiting us, we gathered courage, decided the order in which we should go past him and, above all, to put up a calm front. Pretending that we did not see him, we walked slowly and casually past this soldier. The sentry did not even glance at us. He was staring far out into the sea. His mind was probably on some Japanese island thousands of miles away — his home, wife and children.

Mergui turned out to be quite different from Victoria Point in many respects. This was quite a big town with good roads and strong masonry buildings. This place was truly cosmopolitan. Indians, Burmese, Chinese and I thought even some Siamese were residents here. There was little risk of being identified. The immediate task was to make some local contact.

We set about walking the streets. There were many Indian shopkeepers. One of the shops was a big cutlery and crockery store, which must have been doing good business. We boldly walked in and soon came to know that the proprietor was from the south-east coast of India. His staff were also either his relatives from India or from the vicinity of the owner's village. Had we come a little earlier, we just might be invited for a genuine South Indian lunch. He might still have arranged a sumptuous meal for us had we confided to him that we were the three hungriest men in town. False pride, I confess, defeated hunger, but by a very narrow margin.

We were entertained, however, to some snacks and tea. We talked at length, tactfully parried all awkward questions about our antecedents with elusive replies. Relative strength of Japanese and the Allies, how and when the war was likely to end, whether Japanese rule would be preferable to British Raj, were all the subjects that appeared to deeply interest this well-to-do businessman. We supplied information regarding conditions in occupied Malaya and the attitude of the Siamese. He listened to us with considerable attention. The three of us felt that we were entitled to the welcome dinner and the arrangements made by his Muslim employee for us to spend the night. We had a room to ourselves and clean beds to sleep on. Truly, I pondered, if one was lucky, wealth was not that important.

One member of the staff belonging to the crockery shop took a lot of interest in our future plans. He had accompanied us in our small walks along some of the roads. He told us that there was some sort of land route in a northeasterly direction, which led to Siam. We were not least bit interested in going backwards.

Indians in Mergui were mostly Tamilians, merchants and bankers. There were some Telegu speaking labourers. The cutlery merchant was certainly experiencing depression in his trade, but did not appear unduly worried. The war, though economically damaging, was really too far off to be life threatening. The town had virtually been by-passed by the rapidly advancing Japanese. The interest of the inhabitants was very localized. They were interested in happenings around Tavoy and expected an early restoration of communications to it.

We were advised that the road up to Tavoy was deserted at that time and local bandits hostile to Indians frequented the route. It would be considerably safer and easier to go by bus and the bus service might commence again soon. Eager to get on, we decided to take to the road, however dangerous. Up to now, we had confronted many troubles and faced many risks. While on board the sailing boat, we were soaked to the bones when the rains caught us. There were, however, spells of sun and wind. One got dry fairly soon. Though each of us owned only two shirts, two dhoties and a cloth bag to carry the change of clothing, the weather did not trouble us too much. Also, we had been very regular in taking the prescribed doses of the Atebrin pills.

Our stay at Mergui lasted less than 48 hours. The three of us started for Tavoy early in the morning of the second day. We were not unduly alarmed at the prospect of a long walk — nearly 159 miles. We had anticipated that there would be longish treks. This was obviously the beginning. If we were lucky, after Tavoy we may get vehicles to travel on. We had been told that there was more traffic North of that town than there was from Mergui. True, we could not boast to being in perfect health, slightly debilitated as we were by the travails of the journey up to Mergui. But we derived considerable satisfaction in being free from any specific ailments. Our first anxiety was our protection against the bandits. We had a simple plan. Immediately on sighting any one on the route, we were to scatter into the forests on either side and keep advancing parallel to the road.

Till now, we have had to keep our discussions brief and in whispers. Now with nobody around, we could talk loud and clear and for as long as we wanted. So we did just that. This served two purposes — one, we tended to forget the tedium of the journey and second, we got to know intimate details about one another. It was indeed very surprising how little we had known about each other. Now, there could be no secrets among the three of us. Bit by bit, pieces of our early lives were narrated. During the next few days we had talked enough and all three of us knew about the others' school days, college lives, and subsequent experiences.

In our common treasury, we had a grand common sum of two rupees and a few paise more. It should be enough to last us to Tavoy at least, we reckoned. We were anxious to reach there as quickly as possible, before we ran out of money. We were walking fast. The tall Radhakrishnan, was taking long, steady strides. Natarajan's old ankle sprain acted up and he started to lag behind. It turned out that my normal walking speed put me at a convenient middle between the two.

We took several little rest stops so that we could set off together again. I later wished we had enjoyed more of these breaks. We met only few men on the way. Invariably they were walking alone. It was soon obvious that the report about bandits had been very exaggerated. We were not troubled by any on this stretch. Occasionally, we passed groups of huts on the roadside. These were all totally deserted. We passed, however, two small villages each boasting of a few thatched houses. There was a tea stall in the first one. Rashly we went past it hoping to find a similar establishment at the next village. Here there were a few people moving about, mostly women folk. These appeared to be Telegus (Telegu speaking inhabitants of South India) of the coolie class. It was highly improbable that they indulged in the luxury of tea drinking. We continued our journey after a brief halt under a tree on the roadside. It was a warm day and since breakfast we had not eaten anything. Infact, in order to stretch our money we had decided to eat on alternate days. By dusk we reached a very small village. Totally exhausted, Radhakrishnan and I decided to call it a day and slumped down on the roadside waiting for Natarajan, who was about a furlong behind us.

Within a matter of minutes, I started to feel uncomfortable. I entered a hut and lay down, shivering with cold and my condition seemed to be worsening. I was worried. Was it malaria? Were the Atebrin pills I had been taking regularly useless? Or was it something more serious? What would happen next, with medical attention probably 100 miles away? Of course Natarajan, being a medical man, would diagnose me. But he would be able to do precious little as his pack of medicines contained nothing but anti-malaria pills. I was fully conscious and was imagining the worst. I was indulging in self-pity. I feared that my attempt at escape would be cut short in the wilderness of Burma. Escaping was my idea, yet I am the first one to collapse, I thought bitterly. "Ask Natrajan to hurry up," I told Radhakrishnan, who was looking at me anxiously. My speech seemed slurred.

Natarajan arrived at last. One glance at me and he asked me to get up and come out. My teeth were chattering, my answers must have been unintelligible. I made no effort to move. He was talking to me in an abrupt manner. He went out and returned shortly afterwards. I was then assisted and persuaded to go beside a well hardly ten yards away. Without any further talk he set about trying to cure me without any medicine. His treatment was very simple. He removed my clothes and poured several buckets of water on me. As I spluttered in indignation, he began toweling me vigorously. Slowly the shivering ceased and after sometime I felt almost normal again.

It was evident that there was no question of buying any food. The place was so dirty we couldn't think of eating anything there. In spite of the gnawing hunger and weary limbs, my mood was brightening. When Natarajan explained what was to me a miracle cure, the sheer simplicity of it awed me as much as my total ignorance of elementary physiology. I realised that the shivers had nothing to do with the clear evening in June, almost at sea level in the tropics. The real reason was that we had marched on an empty stomach nearly 29 miles with very few halts. The pores on my skin had dilated too much to keep my blood warm.

The dash of cold water had shrunk the pores to normal size and, eureka, I was whole again!

We then decided to have something — if only a cup of tea everyday. We also decided not to push ourselves too hard, and aim at walking distances not exceeding 25 miles a day. We spent the night inside the deserted hut and set off northwards again early in the morning.

Every Indian we met urged us not to proceed further, as Burmese dacoits, armed with guns abandoned by the retreating British army, had been way-laying travelers specially Indian. The deep-seated resentment of the Burmese people against Indians immigrants, who dominated Burma's trade and commerce, had erupted into violence when the British withdrew. Many Indians had been killed and the relations between the two communities were now very tense. These warnings, added to the ever-present fear of being caught by the Japanese, and hung like a black pall over us. I began having recurring nightmares. Japanese fighter planes would swoop down to machinegun me in a trench, or a circle of Japanese soldiers would grimly close in on me. Just as they were about to thrust their bayonets into me, I would wake up trembling.

After some eight miles or so we fortunately came upon a village on the roadside. There was an Indian Muslim running a tea stall. We had a cup of tea. We were heartened to hear that Palaw was only some 10 to 12 miles ahead. Refreshed and cheered we stepped ahead, but this time with greater frequency of rest stops. We reached Palaw in the afternoon. It was possible that we could have covered at least another 5 or 6 miles that day. When the locals told us that the next village was Palauk (Chota) some 20 miles away, we decided to rest where we were and travel the next day. Immediately on arrival, we had regaled ourselves with one cup of tea each. After some discussions, it was decided that we might as well have some solid food, especially as there was a 20 mile march ahead of us the following day and there were no prospects of our obtaining food or even tea on the way. We had a refreshing bath. Our dinner consisted of a small plate of rice and some daal (lentils) curry poured over it. We allowed a glass of water to make us feel full. We settled down for the night on the verandah (an open porch or portico, usually roofed, along the outside of a building), which was nearly at road level. There was a roof overhead, so even if it rained during the night, there was some protection.

The rest of our journey was uneventful — no bandits and no serious inconveniences. This part of our trek took another three days and our expenditure on an average was being restricted to the prices of a meal and a cup of tea per day per person. We reached Tavoy safe, sound in health and solvent. We met a South Indian, possibly a poor employee under contract, who guided us to a shelter where we could spend the night.

Next morning's breakfast reduced us to paupers. The royal feast consisted of two rice pancakes, bought on the roadside from a woman whose customers were all kings of the roads — the labourers.

Some Tamilian immigrants in Burma from Coimbatore district in South India were contracted as employees of a firm dealing in rice. These friends were not very rich, but the influence of Natarajan, hailing from the same district, was of no little importance. These employees treated us as one of their own. They lived a dormitory life and there food and shelter was available to the three of us. Having been practically starving the previous six days, we must have eaten like gluttons and the result was diarrhoea. The sleeping room was more than good enough for our requirements, but even in my impoverished state, I felt that the latrine was far from hygienic. Being in the midst of a built up area, this fact assumed great importance, especially when one's tummy was running. Our new friends at Tavoy were solicitous for our conveniences. In their company we visited some other residents of the town. On one of these visits, I got an opportunity

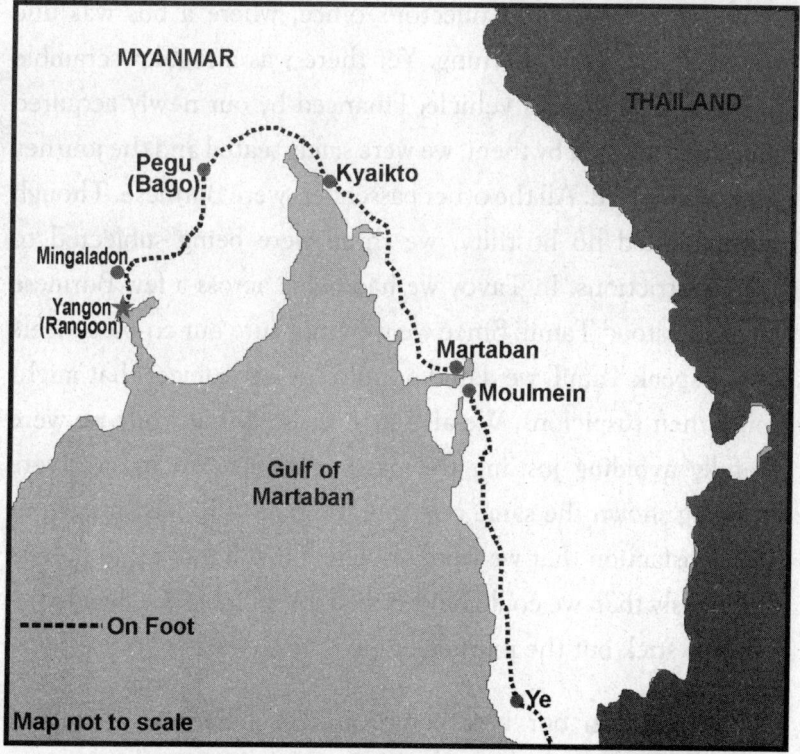

Fig: 4.2 Escape Through Burma (Myanmar)

to look at a school Atlas lying in the house, the first picture of Burma since leaving Singapore. Though the details on the map were meager I certainly found it possible to make some vague plans. I zeroed in on Akyab as the next big stop, a station that would bring us closer home.

We spent some four days, I think, at Tavoy. We had no expenses to incur on our board and lodgings. This rest was to a certain extent enforced on us by our tummy upsets. When we felt our systems were behaving, our restlessness returned. The possibility of being able to travel by a bus up to Ye decided the issue.

We went near the Collector's office, where a bus was due to start. It was early morning. Yet there was a regular scramble to secure seats on this vehicle. Financed by our newly acquired friends and assisted by them, we were safely seated and the journey soon commenced. All the other passengers were Burmese. Though they exhibited no hostility, we three were being subjected to severe restrictions. In Tavoy we had come across a few Burmese who understood Tamil. Since we were not sure our co-passengers did not speak Tamil, we dared not discuss any subject that might arouse their suspicions. We also soon realised that while we were carefully avoiding jostling the passengers next to us, we were not being shown the same courtsey. Be that as it may, it gave us great satisfaction that we were travelling much faster and far less hazardously than we could have hoped for on foot. We decided to patiently stick out the journey.

We were on our best behavior, trying hard to ingratiate ourselves to any co-passenger who glared at us, indicating annoyance probably even on imaginary offences on our part. Yet luck ran out on us. The vehicle developed engine trouble. When the repairs took time, we as well as the other passengers alighted to stretch our stiff limbs. The bus started and stopped a number of times. Along with many other passengers, we tried to push the bus to make the engine start, but to no avail. I knew by then that this bus needed serious repairs before it would start.

We decided to keep pushing the bus so that no one could accuse us of non co-operation. Being in poor physical condition, Radhakrishnan stopped pushing for a while to take a breather. A Burmese, obviously uttering threatening words, caught him and tried to push him towards the bus. Our companion angrily tried to free himself. The Burmese pulled out a revolver and started brandishing it about. This struck awe into the hearts of one and all, except the indomitable Radhakrishnan, who gave vent to his rage in steaming hot Tamil. Luckily, no one understood.

I do not know whether the pistol was loaded or not. Natarajan and I cautiously approached the man acting all nice and humble. Through gesticulations we tried to convince him that we two would exert more to compensate for Radhakrishnan. Whether the rowdy understood us or the steam had all gone out of him, we will never know. He seemed to have calmed down and peace was restored. After that, everbody gave up pushing the bus. We three sat down by the roadside, while the passengers talked excitedly with the driver. It was clear we were dependent on our feet. Most of the passengers started to walk away. Even the driver left, abandoning the bus.

After a short rest away from the madness, we commenced

our journey on foot. We reached Ye on the third day, almost at dusk. We came across a Tamilian who guided us to the house of a Chettiar, a banker. He was very kind and sympathetic. We had dinner at his place and, for some unknown reason, he made us move to a farmhouse in the middle of the night. Very early in the morning, a bullock cart dropped us off near the railway line terminating at a demolished bridge, not very far from Ye. Our guide showed us the direction to reach the road for Moulmein. Thankfully, the journey once again proved uneventful. We covered on an average 26 to 28 miles a day. Our sustenance was again a plate of rice a day and a cup of tea, if we felt we could afford it. We reached Moulmein at about 5 PM. We had no difficulty in contacting our countrymen residing in the town.

A certain Chettiar, said to be a well to do banker, was our choice. When, however, we pitched a tale of being three Tamilians bound for Rangoon, there was not much sympathy forthcoming. I am sure he believed we were harmless individuals. Yet he was least interested in helping us. He was very tight fisted, refusing to part with any cash. The only items of some value left with us were my diamond ring on my finger and the service pocket watch, which somehow had remained in possession of Natrajan till then.

Our offer to sell them found favour with this banker. Astute businessman that he was, he bargained hard to beat the price down. My diamond ring which by now offered no resistance to come off the finger, fetched us eight rupees and the watch another three rupees. In my entire journey this banker stands out alone as a man utterly lacking in sympathy and compassion towards his countrymen in dire straits.

May be my judgement of him is rather harsh. He was only an agent of his master, and he repeatedly said he could not gamble with his boss's money. Besides, he did feed us that night — and no payments demanded. We were informed that a ferry service operated between Moulmein and Martaban across the Salween River, which at this point was miles in width.

The first launch to cross the Salween the following morning conveyed us to Martaban. Inspite of the early hour the boat was crowded. There were a few Japanese soldiers among them. Very little notice was taken of them. We three sat by ourselves next to a bunch of Indians. We soon noticed that no one bothered about us. The vast expanse of water almost inland was fascinating to watch. When the boat touched shore there was a scramble to disembark. Obviously the passengers were in a hurry to get on with their business. We were in no such frantic hurry, but neither did we want to stand out by being all by ourselves. Mingling with the crowd, we reached the railway terminus at Martaban.

Unlike the south of Moulmein, here there was hectic activity, more than on the southern bank of Salween. It was highly unlikely that three Tamilians walking on this busy, crowded road would arouse any suspicion.

All the same, we decided to take the rail line route to Rangoon. Walking along the railway track, we stubbed our toes against the road metal. We started to walk on the sleepers and soon developed an easy rhythm, stepping from sleeper to sleeper. One or two people crossed us on this track and we overtook the odd man going in the same direction. Most were Indians.

It was gratifying to see the great demolition work of the Allied sappers on this track. Every bridge, big and small, had been thoroughly destroyed. Except at Sittang, both the abutments of every bridge had been completely destroyed and the steel girders beautifully twisted and dropped into the waterways. There was no attempt at restoring this line of communication. Except for having to walk bare foot every day, we had no grounds for complaint. There was considerable human activity at periodic intervals along the line. Naturally, there was at least a village near each railway station and many more in between. Every village had a Muslim teashop or a small hotel, where one could buy a meal for three or four annas. If only such facilities existed all along the route and if we were sure of finding money at the rate of one rupee for all the three of us per day, we would have reached Rangoon with some cash in hand. Even allowing ourselves a ceiling of 12 annas per day, we were nearly broke and nearly a hundred miles away from our destination. As things stood, we did not have enough money even for a meal a day.

There was, however, an easy way out. A handful of peanuts washed down with some water seemed to keep the wolf at bay, though very much in sight. This system did not really slow us down. But the weather was causing us some concern. It being close to mid June, clouds would frequently burst into rain. If the showers were short, our body warmth soon dried the clothes on us. We decided to put all these minor problems aside and concentrate on getting to Rangoon.

One day, towards the beginning of our journey, we found a middle aged man and a little girl, around eight, following us. We thought of stopping and talking to him. But he seemed unwilling to come closer to us than a 100 yards or so. Our curiosity was aroused. Who was he? Had he been a 'highway man'? One look at us and he would have gone off after richer prey. He was a Tamilian. We remembered having seen him sometime during the previous night halt.

Our mutual suspicions were soon cleared. It was true he had not only seen us the previous night, but he had overheard our conversation and learnt we were bound for Rangoon. He had thought of following us till Pegu, his destination. He was scared to death of being assaulted by Burmese and had been relieved to know that three Tamils were going his way. His intention was to take advantage of this opportunity, enjoy without our knowledge some protection from our presence close at hand. Gradually we fell to talking. It soon transpired that he was one Munuswamy Naidu from my village in Tinnevelly District, and the girl Setha was his daughter. He had left India some 35 years ago and hence knew very little about the people of my village. I mentioned two names of some elderly persons in my village. He had known them in his younger days, though they were long dead and gone. This common link banished any doubts he may still have had about us. Nearing Pegu, he confided to us that he had a large sum of cash tied round his waist and that was why he was so eager for reliable companions on the way.

We reached Kyaikto, having subsisted for two whole days on peanuts and water. We met some South Indian Muslims here who were in the dry fish trade. As peculiar with the traders on a small scale, they were making arrangements for a collective dinner.

While their food was being cooked, we discovered some of them were from Ramnad, the biggest town in the district of that name. The mention of my uncle's name, a well-known personality in that town, was adequate passport to ensure all comforts while in the company of these merchants. They made anxious enquiries as to how I came to such a pass. The answer that I was employed as a clerk in the Income Tax Office at Tavoy and I was now anxious to reach Rangoon seemed to satisfy them.

There was, however a small snag. The smell of the cooking fish was too strong for our quasi-vegetarian stomach, even though we were ravenously hungry. Natrajan did not mind. But Radhakrishnan had been a vegetarian all his life and I till the year 1930. We decided we would accept some cooked rice and make a meal of it. The only other item that was being cooked was that odious fish curry. There was a very pleasant surprise for us. Having learnt who I was and that one of my companions was a Brahmin, these simple and kindly merchants asked us to get busy with our own cooking.

They had shown genuine sensitivity for our feelings and habits. They had gone to great lengths to get us some lentils and vegetables. There was only a mud pot for cooking. So we did the sensible thing. We put every thing into the pot and let it boil. Hunger is a genius of simplicity when it comes to culinary arts.

Community cooking for them was already complete and they could have finished eating long before our food was ready. We were hoping they would understand that we would not be able to stand the smell of fish curry while eating, but that was too much to expect. But, ultimately, we found that we did not mind the smell so much. Besides, it would have been the height of ingratitude after they had gone to so much trouble getting us special provisions and, on top of it, patiently and hungrily waited so that we all ate together.

After dinner, we travelled a short distance in a boat to a place with a cottage. As it was very dark, I could not find out much about the place, except that it was regularly used as a resting place. The cottage we slept in was probably a resting place for the fishermen. These kind men talked to the owner of the cottage and we soon found that the most comfortable and clean part of the premises had been set -aside for us to sleep in. As the place was rather small, a few of them had to sleep out in the open.

I heard one of the men refer to me and my relatives way back home. He was expressing deep commiseration that a young man had come to such a pass. Such commiseration from total strangers gave me considerable solace. During the remaining journey, I had many more occasions to be the recipient of such kindness. What needs to be remembered was that almost all the acts of kindness came from poor people. It is to them that I owe debts of gratitude I can never pay back.

We were woken up at about 4 AM. I was told it was necessary to make an early start. It had something to do with the tides. While we were on the boat it rained pretty hard. But in the warmth of such kind companionship, we couldn't care less about getting wet.

By dawn we were approaching the right bank of the Sittang River, not very far from the scene of one of the bloodiest battles in the Burma Campaign. I had of course no knowledge then about any action during the Allied withdrawal. But hard evidence was there for all to see in the form of the damaged Bridge across the river. Much later in India, I was told that a friend of mine, Capt Sundaram of Indian Medical Service (IMS), was awarded the Military Cross for his gallant rescue of a large number of Gurkha troops.

I never quite found out where exactly we landed on the western bank of Sittang. By then our Muslim friends had virtually taken charge of the three destitute Tamils from the Tensserim Yomas. As far as I can now recollect, we walked miles and miles and halted at a small village. We three were paupers; we certainly did not starve on that day, nor the next.

At Pegu, our saviours bade us farewell and went their way. We went past the town and, after a crossing, came to a Hindu temple almost on the outskirts of the town. It was indeed very comforting to the weary limbs to relax under the porch in front of the House of God. I had never been a serious heretic after I was about 21 years old. Even if I had been a confirmed heretic till then, I have no doubt that the series of incidents on our journey till then would most definitely have brought me back into the fold of believers. It is common knowledge that ignorance is, by and large, the main cause for blind belief. I can not deny even to this day, that I am ignorant of the reasons that led to a lot of our actions. When these actions seemed to lead to something good, I think I may be forgiven for putting my faith in some unknown force that defies comprehension.

Reports at Pegu gave us a lot of anxiety regarding the journey to Rangoon, a mere 45 miles away. We felt inclined to believe that an Indian's life was not safe in the hands of Burmese, especially if he were to be caught in the dark. We thought of starting about 4 AM and covering the entire distance to the capital in one day, reaching slightly after dark. During our stay at the temple, we talked to a Tamilian who strongly advised us against making such a rash attempt. Our only reason for covering the distance in a day was that we were broke. The Tamilian was not sure, but he had heard that there were some Chettiars at Hlegu, some 21 miles away. If only we had met a good Samaritan at Pegu, another Lamba Kaka of Victoria Point, we would have most gladly spent at rest a day recovering from the fatigue of the preceding days.

Early next morning, we were on the highway leading to Rangoon. While on this stretch there were ample proof that reports about the bandits was no idle talk. We saw a number of dead bodies on the road, more than a dozen, bearing ghastly testimony to the presence of murderous highway-men. The battles had passed this area months ago and the corpses beyond doubt were those of the marauders' victims. It was a warm day and walking in the sun sapped our energy. We had given up the attempt to avoid the road surface and walk along the foliage bordering the road when we realised that there was no way our bare feet could avoid the sharp pricks of a maze of thorns. It was about 3 PM when we walked through Hlegu, a small town flanking the main road, which was running almost East-West here. We saw a little rivulet running at right angles to the road, under a bridge. The town was divided into two equal halves by this brook.

It was a hot afternoon and there was hardly any one on the street. Seeing no prospect of a friendly face, and despairing of finding any one to give us a meal, we thought of heading for Rangoon the same day. Almost at the end of the town and to the north of the road, we spotted a temple. There was a compound around it. We saw a well with a pulley to draw water in the compound. There we met a South Indian, who seeing our exhausted condition advised us not to continue the journey that day. This person turned out to be an employee of a local banker.

Weary and famished as we were, the employee's description of his boss gave us the impression that he must be the kindest man alive on earth. Then and there we decided to end the journey for the day. We took a long, cold bath. Fully refreshed, we became more agonizingly aware of our hunger. We retraced our steps some 200 yards or so and reached the house of this banker so well spoken of. He received us very kindly and, late as the afternoon was, quickly put in front of each of us a sumptuous and delicious meal, which I can never forget. He talked to us with sympathy and, sitting on his verandah near the middle of the town, pointed out to us the wooden stockade on the west side of the bridge, where the Allies had made the last ditch attempt, unsuccessfully, to stop the Japanese advance. We sat down to another substantial meal that night, just six hours after the previous feast. This was indeed a most unexpected luxury — God sent. For quite a long time the hungry hours between two meager meals had been 20 to 24 hours. We slept the night at our host's house. He showed no indication that he expected us to leave. On the other hand he pressed us hard to stay at least one more day.

There were some very good reasons for our anxiety to leave the next day. Firstly it seemed a crime to be within a day's walking distance from Rangoon and yet spend that day idly. Secondly, we found the questions of our host about Mergui and Tavoy become more and more searching. Our ingenuity was sorely tried by his pointed questions. I am positive he had no suspicion at all. When we found the cross examination was getting too involved we could always give excuse that we were overcome with fatigue.

The following morning, after a good night's rest and having partaken of a satisfying breakfast, we profusely thanked our host and took his leave. He was anxious that we should reach Rangoon safe and no harm should befall us after that. If he had only known that our destination was far, far beyond the capital of Burma... We were soon on the tarmac road to the Capital.

We still had the papers issued to us in Singapore, Penang, HatYai and Ranong. We started to feel that it would be better to sever our connections with Malaya and Siam, at least as far as the particulars in the papers were concerned. Earlier, we used to look anxiously at the passport photos obtained with such care from the Chinese photographer in Penang. This talented professional did not make any idle boast when he said the picture would become unrecognizable after a month. We were very happy to see that the duplicate copy at Japanese headquarters in Penang would not endanger our safety any more. Nobody could have identified us with those photos. We were positive on that count.

Till we were within some ten miles of Rangoon there was hardly a soul walking on the road. Of course, many vehicles passed us, up and down. We simply stepped aside or sat down for a while. We carefully avoided being seen as a group of three people walking towards the big city.

Even in this stretch of the road, so close to the capital, we saw the foolproof signs of banditry — dead bodies strewn here and there along the roadside. Till then, our marathon walks had given us no serious trouble except exhaustion. But now, walking bare foot on the hot tar road gave us blisters on our heels. We limped forward at a snail's pace. Then we found ourselves walking on our toes. Finding this too strenuous I decided to walk on the entire surface of the sole of each foot. This felt better, but the blisters under the heels had grown bigger than a ping-pong ball. They began to yield under the pressure of the heel and shift to either side with each step. My first thought was to puncture these carefully and let out the fluid, but realised that would allow the dirt into my body, causing far more serious trouble. It was in its own way, amusing when one felt the heel landing softly on the ground and then see a huge bubble attached to the foot, shifting from side to side with every step. Finally, we had to resort to puncturing these wretched bulbous growths with a thorn. We did so one after another, taking care that the punctures were as far away as possible from the area of contact with the ground.

As we neared Mingaladon aerodrome we saw a number of Japanese soldiers walking about. There was also a large gang of coolies engaged in some repair work on the airfield. Talking to some of the coolies, one realised that if necessity arose one could always earn a rupee and a half a day. If one stood in a cue early in the morning, there was reasonable certainty of leaving the work site at dusk with Japanese currency notes indicating their value to a total of Rs 1½. We found out that initially, the labourers had been reluctant to accept these strange notes but, by the time we arrived, they had got quite used to them, as also to the novelty of the paper currency being prepared right in front of them.

We decided to enter Rangoon that night and explore the town. Just as we walked beyond the airfield, there was a commotion. A motorcyclist had lost control of his machine and it was zig-zagging violently. There was also a pillion rider, both Japanese soldiers. We did the only sensible thing we could. We dashed and took cover behind a huge tree and watched with interest the progress of the motorcyclist. The machine was Allied property. It was also clear that the rider had either never ridden a motor cycle in his life or was completely out of his senses. He was turning about wildly, sometimes going slow but sometimes full-throttle, voluntarily or otherwise. There was no question of risking our lives by coming out from behind the protective trunk of the tree. So, for a short while, we forgot ourselves in the thrill of watching the 'adventures of the motor cycle samurais'.

In matter of minutes the show was over. The motorcycle dashed past our tree with a tremendous roar, went off the road and plunged into a pit hardly 50 yards from us on the other side of the road. The Japanese on the pillion jumped off just short of the ditch, picked himself up and looked into the pit where his erstwhile companion and the motorcycle had come to a rest. What followed was in the true tradition of black comedy. The soldier stepped away from the ditch, stood still for a second and, then, broke out in a roar of laughter. Then he walked off unhurriedly towards the aerodrome.

Assuming that we were safe, we came out from behind the tree and went to the ditch to find out what had amused the soldier so much. Both his companion and the motorcycle were lying dead still at the bottom of the pit some 15 feet deep and the cycle was a few yards away, equally motionless. Our medical friend Natarajan was reasonably certain the soldier was dead. I suppose one could credit his companion's laughter to gutter humour.

We three resumed our journey and shortly after lighting up time, we entered the city of Rangoon. It was four weeks since we had left Mergui. Any one arriving after dark for the first time in a big city would find it difficult to contact his friends. We had no such problems and made contact in no time. True, we were strangers in Burma and in Rangoon the first time in search of a sympathetic countryman. What made it easy was that there were Indians aplenty and thousands from South India alone.

In addition to the permanent South Indians residents, there had been an influx of landlords, bankers, school-teachers and the like from mofussil areas. They had found themselves in a minority amongst hostile Burmese at the outbreak of war and had sought strength in numbers by congregating in areas where there were many Indians. Rangoon's South Indian population had therefore increased immensely. The arrival of three Tamilians, poor and penniless and in a state of indigence, did not cause any suspicion. That was good. Even better was the feeling of sympathy towards such people. From way back Moulmein itself, we had been asking who were most likely to help us. Initially the answers were vague, but in Hlegu we came to know of a few people who might be of assistance. We had carefully memorized the directions on how to contact the South Indian community. In the 'Shule Pogoda' area we met someone who gave us further directions. The immediate need was some place where we could spend the night. Food was secondary. It was easy to find a verandah to sleep on.

Early next morning, things were brightening up in many respects. Some Tamilians began talking to us and their power of observation was as acute as their curiosity regarding conditions in Tenasserim area. Seeing our famished condition, hospitality was readily forthcoming. The news of someone who had braved the journey from Mergui to Rangoon was too good to remain a secret for long. Many who heard the story came to seek confirmation straight from the horse's mouth. Very soon we were referred to Nagappa Chettiar, a man of some substance. After listening to our tale, he very generously asked us to become inmates of his establishment. Problems of food and shelter were thus happily solved, at least for the next few days.

Business in Burma had been dominated by South Indians, mainly through remote control. These business barons mostly hailed from the area of Karkai Mudi and surrounding villages in the district of Ramnad. Their activities embraced a wide field of trade and entered even the remotest parts of central and southern Burma. They dealt in banking, agricultural supervision, owned highly profitable rice mills and dealt in real estate. The heads of the firms did not necessarily stay in the country, but came at intervals of a few years and returned to India after a stay of a few months. Most of the business administration had been left to the local representatives, mostly clerks, accountants, and the like, of business firms. These people invariably came to Burma single, but in many instances married locally even if they had a wife in India.

Therefore it is no wonder that the average Burmese resented this community. The local man was fond of leisure, gambling and drinking and had his own code of conduct, which left the woman not just a mere slave but also the breadwinner of the family. It was not surprising that many women seemed to prefer the dark foreigner who had a knack for earning money, acquiring property and, best of all, gave their Burmese wives jewellery and fine clothes. Women married to Indians escaped the drudgery of hard work outdoors in addition to the domestic chores.

Most of the South Indian residents in Rangoon lived in groups adopting a dormitory system, something like men's hostels. Most of the bosses went back to India, delegating responsibility to local representatives at the outbreak of war. Our host turned out to be very influential, the only local representative of a business magnate in India. Aged 50, he was a man of many parts.

Business activities of the South Indians had come to a standstill with the withdrawal of the British. In an upsurge of nationalistic feelings, the Burmese gave vent to their long suppressed antagonism against the Indians. Might became right and consequently possession more than nine points of the law. The South Indian businessmen fled from their business places to gather in big cities. They were anxious to go back to their tasks, provided their safety was not jeopardised. The Japanese were willing to offer all possible assistance, as there seemed to be no possibility of trade becoming normal again left in the hands of Burmese.

Nagappa Chettiar's hospitality freed us from the worry of having to earn our living. It gave us the freedom to wander round to our hearts' content, exploring the possibilities of how to continue the journey that still remained. Though it was not comparable to a Thomas Cook & Sons' conducted tour, we were witness to a sea change in the history of a great city. Right before our eyes radical changes were taking place. One saw the damages caused by Japanese bombing. The famous Rangoon Market had been razed to the ground.

At first, people fled to the safety of Mofussil areas. Then, in turn, anti-Indian feelings led to the influx of more Indians to Rangoon than the number that had left the city. The intervening period had brought about vast changes. Vacated houses had been taken possession of, locked shop premises had been broken into, either to be taken over lock, stock and barrel, or the place swept clean of all goods for sale, as also all movable property. Innumerable pavement stalls cropped up, the peddlers all Burmese. From the collection of articles and the sheer ignorance of the peddlers about the value of items, made it all too clear where the goods came from. We three had neither the need nor the means to deal with these shop looters turned shopkeepers.

Indians, one and all, were very contemptuous of Burmese business sense, or rather the lack of it. Now that the powerful Japanese were holding the elements in check, Indians were very hopeful of picking up the broken strands of trade. So far, they had been eking out an existence in collective community living and eating into the capital that must have been put away with great forethought when the war clouds were darkening the horizon. The Burmese, quite naturally, were equally determined that the Indians should never again be allowed to dominate the business world in Burma.

The Burmese had not taken into consideration how eager the Japanese would be to restore trade in Burma. This was necessary to assure the people that life was fast coming back to normal under the rays of the Rising Sun. The Japanese authority's urgency was far too great for the inexperienced Burmese merchants to cope with.

There was a story current at that time that the Japanese had approached the Burmese leaders to nominate wholesale merchants to take over a shipload of cargo that was being unloaded at the port after paying for them. The wholesalers were ready, but added that they would pay only after the goods were sold. The impatient Japanese had then contacted some Indian merchants, who not only paid the price down in advance, but were also willing to place further orders, provided the Japanese offered some assistance for distribution of stores in upcountry regions, where there was a problem of lawlessness.

A Burmese deputation appeared to have strongly protested against the preference shown to Indians. Whereupon, the story goes, a Japanese official picked up a couple of Burmese leaders and drove them through all the bazaar areas of the city. He then quite rightly demanded to know why, amongst the thousands of signboards, there was not even a single Burmese name. The two leaders returned crestfallen and had to convince everyone why such a deputation could never succeed.

Our eagerness to resume our journey homewards sent us travelling vast distances and brought us in to contact with many people. In our wanderings, we saw the famous Shwedagon Pagoda, the impressive looking university buildings, the Japanese Wireless

Station that was being elaborately camouflaged to escape the eyes of Allied pilots and many more interesting sights. Our contact included a visit to one Arumugam Pillai, a lawyer of some standing and who was held in high regard by the army of occupation. He was living far off from our "rest house" and we made periodic pilgrimages to this man.

This lawyer was a very busy person. Whenever we could catch him, between his varied engagements, we pestered him with our tales of woe and badgered him with queries. Our aim was to collect as much information as possible as to how far we could go from Rangoon and in which direction. "Would you like to travel to India by submarine?" Pillai asked. As we gaped at him, he explained that the Japanese were training Indians as spies and landing them surreptitiously on India's east coast. "But they want tough men," he said, looking skeptically at our under nourished frames. His suggestion came first as a bit of a bombshell, though subsequently we did play with the idea of accepting his proposal.

According to Pillai the Japanese were conducting regular courses to teach the trainees on what to do and how to carry out 'fifth column' activities on reaching Indian soil. Once the surprise had worn off, one began to see some advantages in such a scheme. Though our minds could conjure up all sorts of difficulties, the main advantage appeared to be the fact that there would be a powerful organisation to put us on Indian soil. There was no reason, at that time, to doubt the Japanese capability to carry out the task. Nor did we have any immediate fears that we might be picked up as spies. I had no doubt in my mind that we could establish our bonafides to GHQ, India. We were therefore quite agreeable to give this proposal a fair trial.

The lawyer, thereafter, was talking to us more freely and we realised he was also examining our suitability for such an adventurous assignment. We had so far stuck to the story that we came from Mergui and Tavoy and had come to Rangoon for security. We had long spells of talks with him. One of my companions had, in a moment of impulse, taken the lawyer into a little more confidence than we wanted. It might have been merely to show we were tough enough to take on the long and arduous journey. He had told the lawyer that, actually, we had started from Malaya. He wanted us to draw up a report, as the local Japanese Commander was anxious to know about the conditions in occupied Malaya. Immediately, I saw the danger. When once such a report was submitted, the next step would have been an interrogation. We promised to prepare such a report and left the lawyer. Discussing the situation, we realised we were in a spot. It meant direct and voluntary contact with the Japanese, at least in Rangoon. If we did not hand in the report, our stay in the city would have to be terminated abruptly.

With heavy hearts we returned to the residence of our Chettiar friend, and informed him of our desire to press on towards our homeland. The old man was full of concern and words of advice. Finding us polite yet adamant, he insisted that we should not go beyond Prome. He was certain that Indians beyond must have either already reached India or had perished on the way. He quoted the case of an Indian Army officer who was working as a doctor's assistant; who would be doing that if he could get away to India?

God fearing man that he was, he was anxious to have our journey blessed by powers greater than his own good wishes. He led the three of us to a temple, where prayers were offered on our behalf at his own expense. Just prior to leaving the temple, each of us dropped a four anna coin into the 'Offerings Box' — the coin he had silently thrust into the hand of each one of us. Such sincerity and good wishes from almost a total stranger was a great source of inspiration for us. After an affectionate farewell, we left that gentle soul and made our way to the railway station. We decided to head for Prome as we knew that goods trains were going there daily and, as in Malaya, passengers were allowed to travel in the goods wagons. Buying tickets with the small sum the kindly Chettiar had given to us, we boarded the train. Before entering the train, however, all the passengers had to undergo a preventive inoculation. What was this to protect us from, I never found out.

RANGOON TO MONYWA

The decision to go to Prome was a wise one, under the circumstances. If only one could get near Akyab — the chances of slipping through was good. Akyab was in British hands and Prome was on the way. Normally this stretch by rail should not have taken more than eight hours. On the way there were many halts and a very long one at Paungde. Any anxiety over the unnecessary delays vanished when we saw the trail of destruction the Allies had left behind, powerful even in retreat. I dearly wished to experience an Allied air raid, whatever the danger to us personally.

The population of South Indians in Prome might have been nowhere near that of Rangoon, but it was adequate for our requirements. Coming out of the railway station we found ourselves in the marketing area where all the sales persons were Burmese

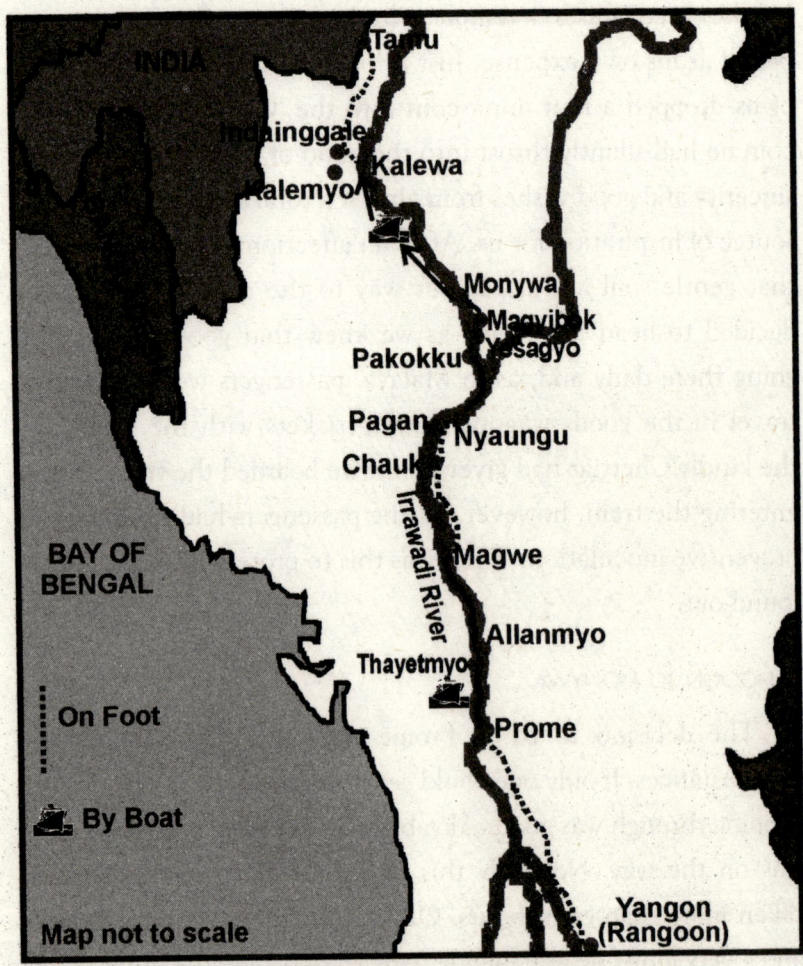

Fig: 4.3 Escape Through Burma (Myanmar)

women. They sat surrounded by baskets containing vegetables, fish, and other commodities. Seasoned by now in picking out the right man to accost, we soon found the prospective host. What helped matters was that the alienated Indians, now frightened of the Burmese, were always glad to meet one of their own.

Food grains were still in plentiful supply. But we had, over time, carefully worked out a simple, but polite, modus operandi, as it were, to assure ourselves the next morsel of food. First, we would befriend a countryman and then wait for an invitation to a meal. The luxury of having our food at no cost, yet at regular intervals started really with the first excellent meal we tasted at Hlegu. This good luck continued during our stay in Prome.

Within a few days one got to know practically every South Indian in the town to form a reasonably accurate impression about most of them. Being unable to pursue their normal vocation, they were willing to while away their time talking freely about matters in general. We three enjoyed the liberty of joining in their talks. They told each other everything about their recent past, what they intended to do in the immediate future — their hopes, ambitions and fears. There were many rice mills, houses and shops belonging to Indian owners who were at that time thousands of miles away. Their local representatives were gradually beginning to see the advantages for the man on the spot. With total control over funds and deals, I am sure some of them at least must have indulged in convenient modes of accounting and recording of incidents to channelise wealth in to their own pockets. Above all, the immense confidence that these people had in their business acumen was self-evident. There was one instance of a banker's representative who was handling considerable amount of cash and administering vast property on behalf of his master. This representative was leading a very comfortable life indeed, till trouble began.

When the anti-Indian trouble broke out, he became the first target in that area. The rice mills under his control were destroyed by fire, his residence was broken into, the iron safes emptied, and he was bayoneted in the belly and left for dead. The wound was still raw with pus oozing out. Immediately, Natrajan asked for some hot water and cotton and began cleaning the wound. Amazingly, he recovered with very little medical aid. When queried, Natrajan found no harm in admitting that he was a doctor. Quite undaunted, and self assured, the man had announced he would recover whatever he had lost in less then a year, if normalcy was restored.

Burma's medical care had been run entirely by Indian doctors. Most of them fled back home once the troubles started. The few that remained moved to big towns. There was hardly any doctor left in Prome and the health of the population was worsening at an alarming rate. Japanese authorities were willing to assist with medical provisions, but there were no medicos to administer them. Natarajan was in a position to be of vital service to the town's people if we stayed back. He himself was very weak because of our long privations and his game leg was causing him considerable pain. Once he recovered he could not resist putting his talents and training to cure the sick. The news of Natrajan's skills had spread rapidly. He was soon in great demand. In fact, so quickly did he slip into his new role that I found him less and less inclined in moving any further. He would ask, "What is the hurry? Why take any more risks when we are comfortable and safe here?"

Bit by bit pressure on him to stay back and heal the sick increased. The reports about the terrain North and West of that area began to have effect. He was more or less convinced that staying a little longer was the right thing to do. Radhakrishnan was not very happy at the prospect of sitting idle in one place. I was getting positively alarmed because the Japanese at Rangoon were still awaiting our report.

The lawyer at Rangoon could have easily ferreted out the information that we three had gone to Prome. If the Japanese suspicions had really been roused, I thought my life wouldn't be worth the Japanese paper money of 24 *annas*. If the Japanese were to get hold of us, the results, I thought would not be very severe for the other two. Radhakrishnan being a civilian, the Japanese could not treat him as an enemy agent. Natarajan's medical status might give him privileges under the Geneva Convention. But my future appeared pretty grim. It was therefore essential that we move on and never stay in one place long enough to be caught. Experience had shown that the local reports tended to exaggerate considerably the perils on the way. We had had ample proof of this in our long trek. Natarajan, on the other hand, felt that I was exaggerating the risks of recapture and seriously under estimating dangers ahead.

We talked with some Hindi speaking Burmese. Some of them were familiar with the route to Ramree in Taungup over a mountain pass. Akyab was only about 100 miles away from Ramree island, indicating we should work our way upto Taungup and beyond over the Arakan Yomas. Further enquiries, however, indicated intense Japanese activity along this route and they were meeting with considerable harassment from the air at the hands of the Allies. One or two Burmese men coming from Padaung across the River Irrawady dashed our hopes. The Japanese were clearing all local people from the area of their operation. Going into such a theatre would be begging for trouble.

Why not try the An Pass? This meant going to the Magwe–Minbu area. At this stage, Irrawady, with its navigation facilities assumed great importance to us. Radhakrishnan and I spent all spare time in getting to the left bank of this vast river and gazing longingly towards the far bank and the direction upstream, i.e., Magwe in the north. There were many boats moored alongside, and we saw some country craft sailing in the river. The boatmen we talked to held out some hope. They were certain that country craft were navigating up north. One boat coming up from further south pulled up alongside the bank for the day. She was to continue

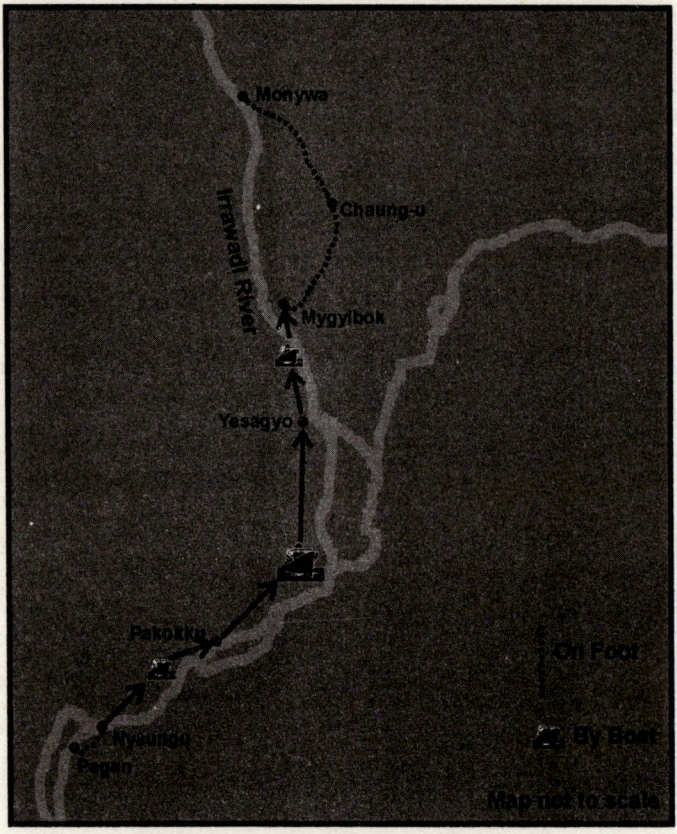

Fig: 4.4 Escape Through Burma (Myanmar)

her journey the following morning bound for Yenangaung, a deserted oil fields area. The man in charge was willing to take on passengers. We soon bargained for our fares, arrived at an agreement and were told to come aboard that night as the boat would weigh anchor early in the morning. We had no difficulty in raising money from our friends in Prome. Sadly, we could not say good-bye to Natrajan as he had gone to a village outside Prome to attend on a case.

The boat crawled slowly up the river, partly aided by the sails. It was hard to reconcile that Natrajan had dropped out. His steady presence had been a source of great strength. His decision to stay back did trigger doubts in our minds. We wondered whether we were being foolhardy in pressing on, and whether we would get across safely even if we did make it to the border. The wind was unfavorable and a couple of the boatmen got down to the bank and patiently and laboriously started hauling the craft up the river. We rarely came across any traffic. A boat came along side ours and its boatman shouted something and moved on. Our boatman immediately altered course and started heading for the far bank. He told us the Japanese were commandeering all country craft and confiscating whatever cargoes were in them. We reached Thayetmyo, to the west of Allanmyo. The boat moored to the jetty, we decided to lie low till things were normal.

We two passengers were entitled to one meal per day even during the period of enforced halt at Thayetmyo. The boatman wasn't bothered. Finding that there was practically nothing to do, I suggested that we walk on to the bank and looked around the town. Radhakrishnan demurred, so I stepped on to the bank alone and decided to spend the day scouting around. It was about 10 a.m. when I left the boat, with a promise to return by noon the following day.

Entering the town, I came across a number of Burmese. There were one or two locals who could speak Hindustani. One of them told me that there was a large number of Indian refugees in some 'busti' or village, some 10 to 12 miles north-west of the town. I thought it would be a good thing to contact them. They might know about some route across Rackam. I left the town about 2 p.m. and by about 5 p.m. I had reached the stream on the way and decided to have a bath and rest.

Suddenly, I noticed a movement in the bushes close by. I first thought it must be some wild animal. Intrigued, I cautiously approached the bush and peered into it. I saw some living thing moving listlessly. I went closer and, to my surprise, I realized that this was no wild animal, but a young girl of about seven or eight years. The moment she saw me, she started screaming and tried to run away. I could see that she was a Tamil girl and I talked to her in her mother tongue. She calmed down a little and allowed me to approach her. The child had a big wound on her thigh and was feverish, probably delirious. She could not talk coherently and did not appear to remember where she was and how long she had been there. I asked her to accompany me to the village where I was going. She agreed, but had great difficulty in walking even with my support. After many halts we were within sight of the village some half a mile away and the sun had already set by then. During the last few hundred yards I had to carry the child. In the twilight, the villagers stopped whatever they were doing when they saw a stranger carrying a little girl approaching. A crowd gathered on the outskirts of the village, almost barring my way.

We were obviously very unwelcome visitors. They did not speak a word as I came within a few yards of the crowd and laid the sick child down on the ground. I told them the child was wounded, sick and probably starving. There was a long moment of silence. I was staring straight at the faces of the people in front of me. A young man very curtly said there was a serious shortage of food in the village. I had no business to bring into this world a daughter whom I could not feed, he added. I told them I was not her father and that I had set my eyes on the child for the first time less than two hours ago. And then I lost my temper and, in rapid fire, no nonsense style, told them how I had rescued the child. I caustically remarked, for good measure, that there must surely be other people in the world who were a little bit kinder then those in front of me. I then demanded some water to revive the child and that I proposed to spend the night under a tree close by, and leave the village for good the following morning.

The crowd thinned down and practically every one went back to their cottage. When I was more or less resigned to the fact that these lost souls would not even give me some water, suddenly a man, well over 60, came with a vessel full of water. I tried to revive the child by washing her face, while the old man stood watching, concerned. Then he started to help me. We carried the semi-conscious girl into the hut and the old man very soon got other inmates to tend to her. After about an hour or so the child quietened down and slept peacefully.

It was supper-time and the last meal of the day was being

cooked. I thought it would be wise to leave the hut to avoid any embarrassment, though I would have appreciated a meal very much. Shortly afterwards the old man came out again, located me and asked me to join him for dinner. I declined, saying I did not wish to be a further burden on the already impoverished community with a meager supply of food grains. The old man would not listen to such nonsense and insisted that I dine with him. He volunteered further that he would look after the child as though she had been a member of his own household.

The meal was simple and frugal — some rice, dal and a curry of bamboo shoots. Spiced, as it were with my host's kindness, the food was delicious.

The rest of the village had practically ignored the visitor and the feverish child and had settled down for the night. After dinner, the old man came out of the hut and spread two mats on the courtyard. Seeing that I was unable to sleep, he started to chat to me. We talked about many things and he asked me many questions. I did not resent it at all because there was no smell of unholy curiosity in the way he asked the questions. My answers appeared to satisfy him. Finding him sympathetic beyond my expectation, I in turn asked him many questions, hesitatingly at first, and later on without any restraint, he answered them all without any reserve. He had been living in the Yenangyaung area and had joined a band of refugees heading for Prome. Burmese goons had forced them to go towards the right bank of the Irrawady opposite Allanmyo. In small, stray groups, the South Indians had found their way to this village. To this day, I don't not know about their means of subsistence and their aspirations.

Some of the old man's friends had gone up north but he could not say if they had got away to India. In all probability, they were still in the area of Monywa. He told me that it was futile to try and make it towards Akyab from Nimbo. Akyab from Thayetmyo? That was impossible. He advised me to go towards Pakokku, and if possible, further north. I had no doubt that this was the wisest thing to do.

The following morning I was getting ready to bid farewell to my kind host. While he was not anxious for me to spend many days in the village, he would not hear of my leaving before breakfast. I therefore joined the family at their breakfast, which consisted of some Appams. I then started back and, after quite an uneventful but tiring journey, I reached my companion on the boat. It was about 2 p.m. The boatmen were kind enough to offer me the meal for the day. I declined, as the rice had already been mixed with the fish curry.

In the meanwhile our boatmen had received some good news. The following morning the boat set sail up the river and we passed safely close to the bank of Allanmyo, but without touching it. There was no sign of the Japanese on the river bank. Hugging the west bank of the Irrawady, we reached Magwe, where we rested. We went ashore to stretch our limbs. There were a number of other boats, and many people were walking up and down. Radhakrishnan had agreed that if there was a way to Akyab from Nimbo, we should leave the boat at this point. We decided to collect some more information about the Nimbo area and the mountain regions towards its west. At this point, we met a Moplah who had just arrived that day from Nimbo and was narrating stories of hardships on the west bank. According to him the Japanese were suffering huge casualties beyond the Arakan mountains. They were keeping all civilians away from the mountain routes, even the Burmese. It was obvious that our chances on this route were practically nil.

We returned to our boat and set off again up the river. The tedious and slow journey was getting on our nerves. Pakokku was still miles away. The restricted rations became very trying. Conversation was also becoming quite an effort. About midday some days later we reached Yenangyaung. The boatman told us that there would be a halt of three or four hours before we moved up the river again. The hustle and activity on the bank caught our attention. We decided to spend the time looking around the town. Needless to say, we hoped to meet someone or at least get some information of some use to us. As we stepped ashore, we found many Japanese on the bank. After overcoming the initial shock, we boldly stepped on and one by one passed the crowd. I am sure the Japanese soldier closest to us did not even notice the bow of salutation we both offered to a representative of his Imperial Japanese Majesty. He was busy looking elsewhere.

For nearly two hours we wandered round. There was not a single Indian to be seen. There seemed to be, however, a lot of training activity. Investing a total sum of four annas, my companion and I treated ourselves to the second meal of the day. A handful of peanuts and a cup of tea each was not only adequate, but thoroughly enjoyable. Any beverage we had tasted since leaving Prome was water.

Despairing of not making any contact, we were making our

way back to the boat. Just 50 yards from the river my companion pulled me up with a jerk and pointed a finger towards our boat. My heart began to sink. There were two Japanese on our boat — one was carefully laying his belongings, obviously preparing himself for a journey on the craft. The other was superintending the loading of some cargo. Boxes of some commodity were being loaded on the boat. Obviously our luck had run out. We did not think it prudent to approach the vessel and enquire which way the boat was going. Fortunately our belongings were with us.

We decided on the spot to find our way to Chauk on foot. It was some 50 miles away and we were quite prepared to spend, if necessary, even three days on this journey. As it was still early in the evening we decided to start right then. After some five or six miles we crossed a small bridge over a river. There was hardly a soul on the way and as it was getting dark we decided to spend the night by the roadside. The following morning we started early and after crossing a village we trudged along towards the town of Gwegyo. Here, there was lot of Japanese activities going on and the local populations were looking at us in an unfriendly manner. Japanese trucks were plying on the main road towards Chauk, so we turned westwards towards the village Sale some 20 miles away. We reached it without any incident and were told that Chauk was six or seven miles off. The sun had set, but we pushed on.

It was about 9 o' clock when we reached Chauk. The town was asleep, and wore a dark, deserted look. Tired and hungry we spent that night under a tree. Our finances were down to a total of six annas. Though we were willing to spend a part of it for a meal, but there was nowhere we could go to buy it. Early next morning, however, there was a certain amount of activity at the northern end of the town, where an isolated teashop in a miserable locality had started to stir. We had a cup of tea each. We were down to four annas. At this stage our aim was to somehow make our way to Pakokku and then onwards to Monywa.

We were told that some boats were plying between Nyaungu (30 miles away along the river bank) and Pakokku. We reached Singu village some six miles North, peopled by labourers. Being fairly exhausted, our first thought was to have a long rest and collect, if possible, all available information about the locality. We had a long rest and the poor South Indians very kindly offered us a meal which they took some time to prepare. Radhakrishnan, being a high-class Brahmin, was debating whether to accept their hospitality or to go hungry. Eventually better sense prevailed and we thankfully accepted the substantial meal the poor people offered.

We decided to recommence our journey only on the following day and spent our night on the verandah of one of the houses. We saw the Japanese carrying out some very peculiar military activities. Singu itself was just a village with two rows of houses on either side of a narrow track, and almost all these houses had been vacated. Practically every one of them was full of ammunition stored by the Japanese, and there was very little MT (mechanical transport) activity. A lot of bullock carts were coming in and out carrying packing cases. Obviously this was an attempt to camouflage a very big ammunition dump and I am sure that the Allies had no inkling of it till we informed them in India.

In the morning we bade farewell to our hospitable hosts. Going past Pagan (Bagan), we reached Nyaungu that night. Pagan was once the seat of the Burmese Empire and its vast ruins told the story of its past glory and the grandeur of its architecture. Coming as if to life in the magical light of the setting sun, the imposing ruins told a tale of epic proportions evoking awe and admiration, for a while making us forget ourselves and our plight.

Nyaungu was, to use the word loosely, modern. All along the road were shops, both large and small, some of masonry structures but mostly wooden huts with tinned roofs. But it was as commercially active as Yenangyaung, though it was much smaller.

In our anxiety to get to Pakokku as quickly as possible (for our total asset now was 4 annas), we made frantic enquiries all around. There were many South Indians and quite a number of Burmese who spoke Hindi. We learnt that the only way to get to Pakokku was by crossing the mighty Irrawady river. This meant money, a commodity we were a little short of. We stayed for two days, wandering round looking for some one to help us. The third day proved lucky. A South Indian was generous enough to give us two rupees. Thus equipped, we indulged in a meal and bargained for a boat to take us across the river. The river was almost like an ocean, a vast sheet of dirty brown water as far as we could see. The bank was so far away it seemed to have sunk into the horizon, yet we were elated that we were just a boat ride off Pakokku.

There were a few other passengers, but all of them were Burmese. One of them was totally drunk and making a scene of himself. When we were about half a mile from the far bank, for some unknown reason the drunkard suddenly turned hostile towards me and brandishing a knife, came jumping at me, shouting "Chetty, are you still alive? I will finish you!" Frightened out of my wits, I dived into the river and chose to swim across rather than face the drunken goon again. Radhakrishnan was standing up, anxiously looking towards me. I waved to him to indicate that I was perfectly alright. I got washed away down stream because of the current, but I had no difficulty in reaching the right bank. After a few minutes, I started looking for some tracks. I soon found a truck junction and taking the broader of the two roads walked along and eventually reached a place which turned out to be Kinla.

Pakokku was some four miles away and the road was good. There were the occasional army vehicles driven by Japanese soldiers, going both ways. Luckily for me one of these vehicles going towards Pakokku had a breakdown and the driver was unable to set the engine right. When I assisted him and got the engine going, he was very grateful and gave me a lift in the front seat. I met Radhakrishnan, on the main road itself. He was searching for me, hoping that I would enter the town by the main road. In the meanwhile, he had contacted one John Babu a Frontier Muslim from India. John had retired in good circumstances and had shown great sympathy to my partner. He took me to John's house, where we were treated like royalty. His advice to us was that the only way to get to Monywa was to go along the river bank at least as far as Yesagyo and then cross to the right bank. He also mentioned that there were a few South Indians families in Yesagyo and beyond. We chatted for a long time, but we could not bring ourselves to tell him that we were broke. While he was very solicitous and gave us wholesome food and two shirts, he never did offer us money. I am sure, however, if we had mentioned this, he would have most willingly given us whatever he could. But our false sense of pride left us penniless.

Next morning we started trudging along the main road towards Yesagyo, some 30 miles away. We were there by night and we had no difficulty in contacting some South Indians. Our first contact turned out to be the wealthiest Indian in the town. He took us home and treated us to a regular feast. We talked late into the night, staying a day longer to recoup ourselves. The following day, accompanied by one of his men, we were taken to the river and the three of us crossed the river half way and landed on a large, farm island. Enquiries revealed that it would be advisable for us to make for the right bank again and head for a place known as Mauale.

From Yesagyo, we were put on board a country-boat that took us to another island in the middle of the river. We spent the night and set off early in the morning after a substantial breakfast, kindly provided free by our host. The same boat took us further up the river and set us down on the right bank in a village called Magyibok.

Monywa proper was still two days journey by foot and it was made clear to us that we could not expect to meet any of our countrymen till we reached it.

Undaunted, we set off on a steady pace along the track to Chaung U, where the track touched the main road from Sagaing to Monywa. We maintained good speed and reached Chaung U by about 4 p.m.

At the entrance to the village we came upon the welcome water-stand so kindly provided by villagers at each point of entry into the village. By then, we felt gnawing hunger.

The village was no more than a small basti with a row of small houses on either side of a thoroughfare. We saw a few locals who merely gazed at us curiously. It was pointless trying to communicate with them. None of them would have known Hindustani.

Our next step was to try and get to the next village towards Monywa some 10 miles away. But after walking three miles or so, we came across a little stream — cool, fresh and inviting. After a wash and drink, weariness overtook us. We decided to rest a while and were soon fast asleep.

When we woke up with a start, we realised that we had overslept and the sun was fast setting. We took the easy way out. We just lay down and slept the night away, with only the empty stomachs to disturb our slumber.

Early next morning, after a 'breakfast' of clear cold water from the stream, we set off. Hunger gave some speed to our weary feet — for food, hopefully, awaited us in Monywa.

Though talking was an effort, we felt the silence around us oppressive. So, we would chat a little, take deep breaths for a while and chat again. We talked about anything that came to our mind — the prospect of a meal at Monywa and conditions likely to be prevalent in India when we got there. The prominent topic was what it would be like in the 'no man's land' just on the Indo–Burma border when the time came to cross it.

At about 3 p.m. we sighted Monywa and elated, we walked faster and entered it by about 4 p.m.

The immediate need was food, then shelter and thereafter some intelligence regarding the territory in the north. Our only hope of contacting a friendly Indian was to scout around the town and hope for the best.

This problem turned out to be more difficult than in other places. Despite our weary state, the two of us kept wandering about wherever our fancy took us. Even by dusk, we failed to make any contact.

Monywa to Delhi

Our sense of elation on entering the town was rapidly ebbing away as we failed to contact any friendly person even after walking miles and miles through the town. Finally, in desperation we decided to make for the river-bank, have a drink of water and spend the night under some tree.

A few hundred yards from the river, we came across a tea stall and gazed longingly at the eatables displayed in front. There were two benches on the roadside. Three Burmese were sitting and chatting loudly and sipping tea. We just did not have the heart — or rather in our case the stomach — to pull ourselves away. The Burmese left in a short while.

Attracted by the two vacant benches, we two gingerly edged up to the bench nearest to us and sat down. We were quite happy to rest our wearied limbs for a little while. We expected the wrath of the tea vendor and were quite prepared to walk away if he decided to shoo us off. But the reception we received was totally unexpected.

We found the tea vendor standing in front of us with two steaming cups of tea. The situation was embarrassing. There was not a pie between the two of us. Radhakrishnan explained that we were merely resting our tired feet and that we had not ordered any tea. I meekly added that we were completely broke.

As the vendor still continued to hold out the cups to us, we gladly accepted the beverage and drank it. Without a word, the vendor went inside and was busy with his pots and pans. We returned the empty cups to the counter and were hesitant to express even our gratitude in words, lest we should disturb our benefactor in his activities.

There were no more customers and probably it was the usual closing hour. The tea vendor retired into the interior of his premises and sat down for his supper with his Burmese wife. We hoped that he might take some interest in us after supper. On the contrary, totally ignoring us, he shut shop and retired for the night.

Two vacant benches were too tempting. We dropped all other plans and decided to spend the night there in front of the tea stall. Our emaciated frames were pressing hard on the wooden bench. Sleep was difficult. The following morning, we woke up fairly refreshed, but our stomachs were still empty. We went to the river and had a bath in its cool waters. We wanted to get back to the tea stall to thank the vendor and to extract information from him. While we were walking towards the tea stall, we finally met a Tamilian. He painted rather a gloomy picture regarding conditions in Monywa.

It would appear that all Indians, particularly South Indians, had left for India much earlier, mostly by the land route. Many had gone down to Rangoon with the hope of making a sea voyage to their homeland. There were only a few Indians left in this town. All the South Indians lived in a particular part of the town and their conditions were none too happy. It had been worsened by an influx of refugees and there was very little chance of our getting any tangible assistance. The only redeeming feature, according to our informant was the tea vendor, a Moplah from South India. Though he himself was poor and was eking out a bare existence, he was very kind hearted.

On returning to the tea stall, the mopla gave us a cup of tea each and this time he was not so silent as on the previous night. He listened to our tale of woe patiently, gave us a lot of information which only confirmed the Tamilian's reports. He made it clear that our proposed visit to the South Indian colony would be pointless. Nevertheless, he gave us directions as to how to get there. We had no difficulty getting there and, after enquiries, called on the most important person in that colony.

This person met us on his verandah and seeing our hungry look, brusquely told us not to expect any invitation for food. The poor man had crossed the limit of his endurance. The stream of refugees sponging on him and his grain supply was rapidly dwindling.

He was a shrewd person and saw through our claims pretty

clearly. He advised strongly against venturing further and insisted that we return to South Burma, whence, he thought, we had originally started. I would not say he was not an unkind man, but the very real fear of penury made him put his faith in one adage: "Charity begins at home". There was nothing further to be gained. So we left him and commenced our wanderings afresh in the town.

At about midday, finding ourselves in the vicinity of a pongycham, we went in to rest for a while. There we came upon two Manipuri Brahmins, who were about to sit for their middy meal behind a cloth curtain. They were kind enough to let us partake of their frugal fare. Our morale went up to some extent. We were quite content to go without food for the rest of the day. Walking back from the pongycham, we noticed a large building on the riverbank, with a Japanese sentry at the main gate. This we learned was the local headquarter of the Japanese Army and aptly looked forbidding.

Without money and without a friendly soul in town, the matter of pushing on further became imperative. Our next objective was Kalewa some 200 miles away.

All information indicated that we had set ourselves an impossible destination. The land route meant traversing jungles full of wild animals. But this did not deter us. Much more frightening was the certainty of armed marauders freely roaming on all the jungle routes. All Indians were marked men as they were reputed to be wealthy ... or carried large sums on their person.

The only other route was up the River Chindwin. Here too,

we came up against a stonewall. Only the Japanese were moving up and down the river and even fishing boats had disappeared as the fishermen were afraid of their craft being commandeered by the Japanese. They were entirely for the Japanese troops and no other nationals were permitted as passengers. The only exceptions were the few Indians from Chittagong with knowledge of the river and their exclusive task was to navigate the power-boats.

After examining the pros and cons several times, we decided to apply for passages on one of the boats that the Japanese were sending out to Kalewa. Had we not succeeded getting our applications accepted at the Japanese headquarters in Penang and Ranong? Why should we not therefore apply to the local military headquarters?

The next morning, we cautiously walked up to the Japanese sentry at the gate and were quite prepared to bow low and greet him with the words "India—Gandhi", a phrase which had worked like a charm in our dealings with the Japanese.

The sentry who was looking elsewhere, did not take the slightest notice of us, and we walked in boldly. The headquarters was housed in a large building with an open and spacious ground in front. There were a few persons sitting round the table on the ground. We stood respectfully some five yards away, awaiting the august personage to take note of our presence. There was only one Japanese officer, with a Burmese and a Manipuri beside him. There was a large map spread in front of them. From their discussions, it appeared that they were collecting information about the India–Burma border terrain from the Manipuri.

In accordance with the role we had assumed, we put on the most blank expressions that we could think of. When the Japanese saw us, he beckoned us closer and we started jabbering in two languages — Radhakrishnan in broken Hindustani and I in Tamil. Very soon a procedure evolved itself by which he did most of the talking with the Manipuri in Hindustani, who in turn translated it into English for the benefit of the Japanese. I put in a few words in Tamil to Radhakrishnan occasionally. The Burmese also occasionally joined in the talks in broken Hindustani.

It was soon evident that by asking for a passage to Kalewa on Japanese controlled boats, we had raised many doubts, which needed to be cleared through interrogation. Fortunately, this was not a continuous process. Our tale was a simple one. We were both new to Burma. My companion had spent some eight months and I had reached Rangoon only a couple of months before the outbreak of trouble. One of my brothers had left for India by the land route leaving the coffee house in our charge. When the troubles reached Chauk, we had abandoned the shop and moved northwards. We had heard that my brother was lying ill in the area of Kalewa.

The Japanese officer appeared to be concentrating on the main problems of his map and hence the interrogations were carried out in fits and starts. In between, more to carry conviction, we pointed out that we were very hungry. The Japanese officer was kind enough to provide us a meal from the cook-house within the compound.

I found one of the workers in the kitchen was a Madras sapper and I began talking to him in Tamil. Soon the officer got annoyed at my talking to his staff and shouted at me angrily. I bowed low and appeased him with my 'humility and innocence'. After some more questions and answers, we were asked to come back the next day.

We visited the Japanese headquarter on three consecutive days and finally managed to obtain necessary permits for both of us to travel by boat to Kalewa.

Before that, the interrogators had contacted Chauk to verify our claims. Authorities in that town replied that there was a coffee house by the name we had given, but they did not know the name of the owners. We were given the benefit of doubt. Indeed luck was again on our side. We were luckier still when the Japanese accepted the last interpretation to suit our version. A slip of paper was handed over to each of us. We just about managed to hide our elation. Just for effect, we asked whether food would be given to us on the boat. The answer was an emphatic 'no'. Thereupon, we pretended sudden loss of interest and I politely placed my permit back on the table, telling them in a resigned voice that without food the permit was useless to us. Without any false modesty, I must say that our performance was Oscar standard and the nice Japanese officer fell for it. He scribbled some thing on the permits and pushed them towards us, saying we would be given food on the boat.

Just managing to mask our feelings, we very politely expressed our gratitude and, Japanese style, bowed low in obeisance. Then we left the place, walking slowly, though what we wanted to do was to run and shout for joy. During the free time in the three days of interrogation, we walked the street of Monywa, discreetly collecting information. We spent the night on a motor boat, moored for repairs.

We occasionally called on the Moplah tea vendor. He was not happy with our having spent two nights on board a derelict boat. On his invitation we spent our fourth night under the protection of his humble abode, which was a tea stall by day and his home by night. It was this kind of people, who showed such concern, kindness and generosity to total strangers and destitutes like us, that kept our faith in humanity alive, despite all the other experiences to the contrary.

The next morning we were at the jetty as we had heard that a boat was due to leave for Kalewa. Radhakrishnan and I were to be the only passengers by special permit. Then the totally unexpected thing happened. The Japanese officer, who was checking the embarking personnel, took a sudden dislike to us. He not only stopped us from getting on the boat but, in a fit of temper, tore up our permits and threw the pieces into the river. All the labour of the last four days floated down the river.

We had to wait till his temper cooled. The native mechanic and the cook failed to turn up and the boat was being delayed. This was to our advantage. The Japanese officer-in-charge asked us whether either of us knew anything about the engines. Of course we knew. Did we know any cooking? 'But naturally', was our response. These answers were our passports. We were on board. The engines were started and we were off.

Our journey up to Kalewa took considerably more time than normal. The navigating party was not sure of the river and we were zig-zagging terribly. At night we stopped. We travelled only by day. Also, for the first time, we witnessed Allied air attacks.

After three days, at about midday, we reached Kalewa and we disembarked. But then came the hitch. We were told to stay ready as our services might be required to move down stream if they did not find the necessary personnel in the town. We pleaded for a short leave to search for 'my ailing brother'. As the return journey was not due for another four or five days, we easily got the permission.

We ate lunch on the boat. No sooner had we landed and got permission to 'prowl around', we set off on the highway leading to Tamu. Our spirits were high. After covering some two miles or so over a winding mountainous road, we came to a promontory jutting out into the river. A stream joined the river to the left of the promontory.

One of the Japanese sentries manning a picket was outside idling his time away. The road was submerged by the stream and on entering the water I realised Radhakrishnan would not be able to cross it. The stream was some 100 ft wide and there was no possibility of my swimming across with him in tow. At this juncture, a Japanese soldier, who was fishing in the middle of the stream, came paddling towards us. We hurriedly prepared ourselves for some interrogation. Luckily for us, he understood our gesticulations and was good enough to take us across the stream on his canoe.

Once across, we walked fairly fast with the intention of covering as much distance as possible. The road to Tamu on this stretch ran across many little streams, all of which were fairly easy to negotiate.

Our route in this area was completely deserted. There was not a soul in sight. Beyond the noise of jungle denizens, it was very quiet indeed. Our voices sounded so loud that we started to whisper.

This was the end of July and the day was quite warm and sticky. When we crossed shallow streams we enjoyed wading through the cool waters. Sometimes, I had to swim across first to check the depth and if necessary, find a shallower crossing upstream for my companion.

These crossings slowed us down considerably. By about 4 p.m. when we had scarcely covered a few miles from Kalewa, we had to cross another stream, which was merely 30 ft wide, but about 8 ft deep at the centre. Nearly an hour was spent in vain looking for a shallower diversion. Upstream, the jungle was very thick and thorny.

On my suggestion, we tore a spare dhoty into strips twisted it and tied the ends together to use as a rope. We tied one end to his waist. I swam across holding the other end and instructed my companion to check the rope around his waist. Then, suddenly, he got cold feet as soon as he entered the water. All my efforts at cajoling and encouraging him to keep going proved useless. He dashed back to firm ground and would not budge. I pleaded with him to put his faith in my capacity to pull him across. He did not budge. He held on fast to a thick bush, so that I could not jerk him up to his feet. He was generous enough to suggest that I go on alone and that he would try to find some other way out for himself.

I was so confident of pulling him safely across, that I became very impatient with his diffidence. Persuasions having failed, it was time for a trick. Suddenly I shouted: "Hey, careful! There is a snake near your feet!" He jumped, letting go of the bush. I immediately caught him and pulled him across the stream without much trouble. I dragged him up on the other side, made him sit up. He had taken in a fair amount of water but was none the worse for it. He was furious and spluttering. After he had become a little more comfortable, he berated me for attempting to drown him. He became calmer, but remained sulky. I suggested that we continue walking in the hope of finding a village for shelter that night.

After some two miles' walk along the Tamu Road, we passed a village on our left. A youngster playing on the outskirts was shouting to us. We did not understand him and kept walking. He persisted running alongside us and kept on yelling *"mat jao, mar jaega."* (Don't go, you will die.)

We were wondering what he was trying to tell us. We were very thirsty and it was late in the afternoon. So we retraced our steps and entered the village.

The village was just a group of huts on either side of a pathway. Walking along this central path, we were the focus of a few unfriendly stares. There was, however, a young man in his early twenties, sitting in the cool shade of his verandah. Lucky for us, he could speak broken Hindustani. Our polite request for drinking water was granted in silence. His young and pretty wife fetched it for us. We asked him the direction to the pongycham of the village, so that we could spend the night there. He obliged.

As we were walking away, we heard some conversation between the husband and wife. Thereafter the young man called us back and was good enough to ask whether we had eaten. We returned to the verandah, and were treated to a sumptuous meal of cooked rice, dal and bamboo shoots.

It was almost dusk. We thanked our host, bade farewell and started walking away. We then heard a hurried conversation between the husband and wife and we were recalled. Without any word of explanation, the young man said that we were permitted to spend the night on his verandah. We thought it was very kind of him. Later our scared minds began to entertain doubts regarding his intentions. We could not understand why his solicitude for us should have extended to such lengths.

The couple had retired for the night. Radhakrishnan and I stretched out on the verandah, a wooden floor about 15 inches above the ground. In a little while we heard some peculiar noises coming from within the house. On cautiously peeping through a slit in the door, we saw a strange sight. The woman was sleeping on the floor. The husband was sharpening a large *dah* (a long lethal knife or half sword of the Burmese) in the light of a hurricane lantern.

We were alarmed. We dared not talk for fear of being overheard. My imagination was running riot and my friend's condition was no different. After offering such hospitality, albeit at the bidding of his wife who was kindness personified, why was our host sharpening a lethal knife in the middle of the night? The two facts were irreconcilable. We two managed to whisper a few words and pretended to be asleep, all prepared for a quick getaway if need be.

A little later, the door opened quietly. In the dark, we saw the couple come out on to the verandah. If the suspense had continued a minute longer, we both would have jumped up and bolted away. But the Burmese had no weapon in his hands and his wife was only carrying a bundle. We realised to our immense relief that it was a mosquito net. They opened it out and tied it over our heads and dropped the sides around us. The couple then silently withdrew into the house and closed the door gently. Our feeling of relief was so great that it took me some time to feel a sense of gratitude for this fine gesture of solicitude.

When we woke up the following morning the host took complete charge of us and set our minds at rest on the food front. Later we came to know that it was at the insistence of the kindly Burmese woman that we were given food and shelter. Just as well. The pongychan would have been a veritable death trap for us, for the South Indians who had taken shelter there had met with violent deaths at the hands of some of the villagers who hated Indians with a vengeance. Our host said that it was not necessary to go all the way to Tamu. The Indian Army, he said, frequently patrolled areas few miles to the east and if we headed in that direction we could run into them. As he was talking, a villager came running. Our host turned to us. "A Japanese patrol is coming" he said. "You better hide inside my house". Dragging a few sacks of rice in front of a wall he made us squeeze in between. It was a flimsy cover and anyone entering the room would spot us immediately. We waited, hearts pounding. An eternity later, the door opened. "They have gone," said our host.

Meeting this frail looking Burmese and his charming wife turned out to be very fortunate for us. He instructed us to remain indoors during the day, gave us tasty, wholesome food three times a day. Above all, he inspired great hopes for our escape by supplying a fund of information regarding the locality.

Indainggale, for that was the name of the village, lay in no man's land. Periodically, patrols visited the village both from Kalemyo in the hands of the Allies as well as Kalewa, in the hands of the Japanese. The main thrust of the Japanese had gone as far as Tamu in the North. The Kalewa garrison was guarding the left flank towards Kalemyo by merely patrolling once in three or four days.

Patrolmen of both the sides had interrogated the villagers. Otherwise, life here was fairly peaceful. There were Allied air raids whenever enemy patrols had been noticed in the vicinity. There was one such raid during our stay but it was only strafing and no bombs were dropped.

I assisted the host in stocking the rice bags and to prepare protective lanes within the house where, in an emergency, the occupants could seek shelter. We were also of valuable assistance to our hosts by treating his ailing child with Altebrin tablets. As luck would have it, the baby had only malaria and the tablets had a wonderful effect.

Our physical condition was tolerable, but the problem of reaching Kalemyo still stared at us. The Allies had, for a while, set up a forward post along the road to Kalemyo.

Midway between Indainggale and Kalemyo was the river Chindwin. But owing to heavy rains, all the way from the village to the river was impassable slush. Usually, there was a ferry system. People brought the boat to the river, crossed it and on return used an elephant to haul the boat back to the storage shed. Elephants could not walk in the sludge and we had no means of acquiring a boat, nor the money for the fare, which, in those days, was exorbitant. Our curative talent came to our rescue. A retired Gurkha serviceman had to be treated for fever and our Altebrin tablets fetched us some money.

Our presence in the village could not be kept a secret. There were one or two local residents who came up to our host and demanded that we should be asked to go. Our host, as the headman of the village, rejected these demands. But we came to know that a Japanese patrol was expected any day.

After a stay of three days in Indainggale, we decided to find our way to the river and explore on the spot the possibilities of crossing. Finding us firm in our intent, our benefactor gave us some money and wished us a safe journey. We reached the river-bank one morning after wading through a couple of miles of slush. One look at the river was enough to make Radhakrishnan's heart sink. There was no ford, no easy way to cross. We finally decided to build a raft, with torn strips of cloth and timber pieces salvaged from a dilapidated hut on the bank. The width of the river at the place would have been about 50 yards and the current was feeble. As a last resort, I could swim across, hauling the rickety raft with Radhakrishnan on top. But he was morose throughout our activities, as he did not believe the raft could carry us across. Just then, a party of three men and an elephant hauling a country boat came to the bank and were preparing to go across. We appealed to the boatman to give us a ride. In a jovial mood, he asked us to hop on. In a few minutes, we were on the other bank. When we thanked the boatman, he responded by returning half the fare and waved us off. We were left speechless.

As we walked on, we saw a road going up the mountains and there was a signboard with an arrow pointing the direction to Fort White — a British Camp.

As we came nearer the camp, some Indian soldiers appeared, told us to stop and came up to us, guns ready. There was a Sikh havildar leading the patrol. We almost jumped with joy. "Who are you?" the Sikh challenged us.

"I am an Indian army Officer," I replied.

Seeing his surprise, I added: "I was in Burma fighting and got lost". I did not want to say that I had come from Singapore because I knew he would not believe me. Even so, he looked dubiously. I don't blame him. Thin, scraggy bearded, barefoot and in a faded shirt and dhothi, I must have looked a sight.

"What was the name of your Unit and its formation?" he asked. I said nothing. The havildar sneered. "I have seen a lot of people like you trying to sneak into India," he said, adding, "An army officer indeed!"

"I am an officer. Take me prisoner if you like," I said.

The havildar spat, "I have come here to kill the Japanese," he said, "not to take prisoners. Now go back".

When I heard those words, something snapped in me and I started running. A machine gun spattered and stone sprayed around me. I stopped, turned around and started cursing the havildar in fluent army Hindustani. I raged on. The havildar was dumbfounded. Only a real army officer would have had the temerity to curse him. Producing a note book, he asked me to write down my name, rank and Unit. Then, pointing in the direction the patrol had come from, he told us that there was an army camp a few miles up the path. An hour later, we stumbled into it.

Three months and two days after leaving Singapore, we were free and safe at last. Things moved with dizzying speed after that. Word was flashed to Army Head Quarters of the arrival of the first prisoners of war to escape from Singapore. The British Officers contacted Delhi through wireless. We were provided with houses and runners for travelling over the mountains and we reached the city of Aizawl, the headquarters of the British Commissioner. With his assistance, we went on to Silchar, reached Calcutta by the Assam-Bengal Railway, crossing the Brahmaputra. From Calcutta, we were flown to Delhi, and finally, I reported at the Allied General Headquarters. There was, at that time, a total lack of information regarding events in Singapore since its fall on Sunday, 15th February 1942. Quite naturally, the Directorate of Military Intelligence at Delhi was extremely keen to gather every bit of intelligence regarding Malaya and Burma under Japanese occupation. For them, I was the first man with first hand knowledge about these countries, as also the only one who had directly dealt with the Japanese.

The interrogation by the Officers of the Military Intelligence Directorate was exhaustive. The Director, General Hawthorne, sat in for a couple of hours every day. On two occasions, the Commander-in-Chief, General Wavell himself, was a silent participant in the proceedings.

On General Wavell's personal recommendation, both Radhakrishnan and I were awarded the Military Cross.

EPILOGUE

It was a fine day in September, 1942 that I had the privilege of being summoned to meet no less a person than General Sir Archibald Wavell, MC, the then Commander-in-Chief of the Indian Army.

On 7–8th December 1941, Japan launched the first offensive against the Allies without a declaration of war. Within the next three days, the unsinkable *Repulse* and *Prince of Wales* had been sunk off the Malayan Coast. Hongkong fell easily into Japanese hands. By the end of January, the Malayan campaign was virtually over. Singapore, the bastion of the British empire in the Far East, could not stem the onslaught of the Japanese army. The British Empire was rocked in its fundament.

On Sunday 15th February 1942, in the afternoon, the Malayan Command had surrendered the island to the enemy. From that date onwards, there was practically a black out of information in India regarding the last stage of the campaign and the plight of Allied prisoners in Japanese prison camps.

At the time of its fall, there were more than 75,000 Allied troops in Singapore. There was naturally great anxiety about them in the High Command and the civil administration in India.

Hence, it was not surprising that the General was keen to meet an Indian officer who was the first person to reach India after having taken part in the Malayan Campaign and, to add to it, had experienced life in a Japanese prison camp.

The Directorate of Military Intelligence at GHQ, New Delhi was anxious to make the most of this opportunity. They took almost three weeks to collect all the information they could get through detailed interrogation, from the first available source. Finally, the interrogation was over and I was taken to General Wavell for farewell. His informality put me at ease, as did his kind interest in seeing me recoup my health. Our conversation went something like this.

General Wavell — Where do you come from, young man?

Pillai — I come from the extreme south of India, Sir, you would not know that area.

General — Never mind the extent of my ignorance. Where exactly is your home?

Pillai — I belong to Tirunelveli, Sir, very near Cape Comorin.

General — I know that area a little. I was very nearly drowned while swimming off the coast. A fisherman come to my rescue and pulled me on to a catamaran. I was then a subaltern.

Emboldened, by his letting me have a peep into his early life, I said — "I am a Tamil, Sir, and I belong to the non-martial classes."

General — "Non-martial classes, my foot — you have beaten even the Pathans. I reckon, that yours should be the record now, in the matter of escapes. I am not aware of any escapee having traversed nearly 3,000 miles of enemy occupied territory."

I was thrilled to hear such words of praise from India's highest ranking soldier. He talked to me a little while longer and then left me to be taken care of by his staff officers. I had many such interviews with the august personality. He wound up the final meeting by saying: "Your experiences were such that in my old age, I could sit by the fireside, stick a pipe in my mouth, put my feet on the foot stool and tell [your] story to my children and grand children".

According to him, I had enough material to write a book, but he warned: "Write it after the war is over."

My partner in the 3000 mile adventurous journey, Radhakrishnan, a civilian, was a lecturer in the Singapore Trade School. As entry into Allied lines was highly restricted, I had to introduce him as a member of the Allied Armed Forces, a subaltern in 'Singapore Volunteers'. The well-meant lie did result in a perplexing situation, but the result was 'jolly good', as our Sandhurst crop of officers would put it.

The C-in-C had promptly put up both our names for the Military Cross, and with remarkable speed the decorations were published in the *London Gazette*. While there was no hitch in checking my antecedents, Radhakrishnan's parent unit could not be traced, for the simple reason that no such unit as Singapore Volunteers existed. I confessed to them that there was no other way I could have brought him with me into Allied lines. I am sure this is the only instance of a civilian being decorated with the Military Cross. It did not matter very much, I think, as he was commissioned into the Corps of Engineers and was posted, albeit on paper, to the Royal Sappers and Miners, my parent Regiment.

During the following few months, when I was gradually recouping — my weight at that time was less than 90 lbs, 64 lbs less than it was before becoming a prisoner — I had ample leisure to ponder over the advice of General Wavell. I decided to put on paper everything I could remember while it was still fresh in my mind.

I wrote an essay titled "Three Thousand Miles to Freedom" while I was at Staff College, Quetta in October 1945, a synopsis of my escape. The comment on my essay, by the General, the then Commandant of Staff College was: "A good story, well told. I would have found it even more interesting if you had shortened the account of the preparations and told us more about the actual journey."

After the end of World War II, there were questions asked as to whether my experiences would be of as much interest as the other books, especially those published by people who joined the Indian National Army (Azad Hind Fauz) of Netaji Subhash Chandra Bose. When I left Singapore in May 1942, there was only a formation called the 'Indian Independence League' and we got its membership cards. The INA (Indian National Army) had not yet been formed.

I have often wondered what makes some people go in for dangerous, risky ventures, out of the ordinary run of life. Is it a strong sense of duty? Or is it a powerful instinctive urge for thrills and adventure that will not be denied? Prior to my escape, I was a member of an organised force defeated by a superior enemy. I was still entitled to wear my uniform or what was left of it and could feel a certain amount of security in strength of numbers. My brethren in distress were over 75,000 in number. My responsibilities towards my men were not very great, as I was at that time near the bottom rung of the ladder.

To this day, I have not ceased attempting to analyse the reasons that forced me to leave such a position and seek freedom by undertaking a fairly long and rather difficult journey. The experiences are so deeply etched into my mind that I have no difficulty in recalling them — at least the important ones.

It might be that I was deeply moved by the stories of heroism, which I had read in my earlier days. Again, I am well aware of the recklessness of my youthful days and the high opinion I had of myself. It is equally possible that my sensitive nature of those days had been stung to the quick too often by numerous jibes at 'a rice-eating South Indian of small physique' and I was anxious to prove that I could also take my share of physical hardships.

Yet a few soldiers, a very few, managed to get away from Singapore and among them was 2nd Lieut. M.M. Pillai of 45 Army Troops Company. Here is how I would put the whole affair in a nutshell.

Pillai, a Tamil from Southern India, escaped from his prisoner-of-war camp in Singapore. Suitably disguised, he mingled with the local population. With his two partners, Radhakrishnan and Natarajan, he made his way to Penang where, claiming to be a merchant, he obtained a passport from the Japanese Headquarters to leave Malaya. They managed to get a visa to enter Burma from the Japanese Consul at Ranong, a Siamese port. They made their way slowly to Prome *via* Mergui, Pegu and Rangoon. Around this time, Natarajan decided to stay back. The efforts to get to Akyab did not succeed. He and Radhakrishnan therefore worked their way up the Irrawaddy as cooks in a boat manned by the enemy and, on reaching Northern Burma, took to the jungle. There they marched for three weeks, sick and starving, until finally they reached the Allied line near Fort White. For this exploit, the two were awarded the Military Cross.

EDITOR'S NOTE

Six months later, three other Indian officers escaped from Singapore prison camp and made it to India. As far as is known, none of the other 88,000 Allied POWs in Singapore escaped. Radhakrishnan was subsequently commissioned into the Army. He died in 1945 of complications arising from the strains of the journey. Pillai retired from the army as a Brigadier in 1961 and lived in Madurai till his demise. He was never able to re-establish contact with the third fellow escapee, Natarajan.